Adorn Yourself with GODLINESS

A Study of 1st Timothy and Titus

How could you be more beautiful than to adorn yourself with the very character of God so that your life displays the beliefs you claim to profess! You can choose to "dress," act, and be like Him — for Him!

Melanie Newton

JOYFUL
WALK
BIBLE
STUDIES

We extend our heartfelt thanks to the many women who served as contributors to the original version of this study guide, especially Joan Floyd, Liz Church, Lori Schweers, and Penny Semmelbeck. For this updated version, we are grateful to Nancy Stephenson, Julia Gendron, Kim Newton, Vanessa Morris, Lida Lowey, Aimee Jones, and Heather Newton for your great job of editing the lessons. Your contribution to this study is much appreciated.

Adorn Yourself with Godliness: A Study of 1ˢᵗ Timothy & Titus

Published by Joyful Walk Press. Flower Mound, TX.

ISBN: 979-8-9925303-3-9

For questions about the use of this study guide or for bulk orders, please email us at melanienewton.com/contact.

Cover image is a public domain image of a vanity found on www.maisonsdumonde.com.

Melanie Newton is the author of "Graceful Beginnings" books for anyone new to the Bible and "Joyful Walk Bible Studies" for established Christians. Her mission is to help women learn to study the Bible for themselves and to grow their Bible-teaching skills to lead others.

Joyful Walk Bible Studies are grace-based studies for women of all ages. Each study guide follows the inductive method of Bible study (observation, interpretation, application) in a warm and inviting format.

We pray that you and your group will find *Adorn Yourself with Godliness* a resource that God will use to strengthen you in your faith walk with God.

Christ-Focused • Grace-Based • Bible-Rich

JOYFUL WALK PRESS
Flower Mound, TX

MELANIE NEWTON

Melanie Newton is a Louisiana girl who made the choice to follow Jesus while attending LSU. She and her husband Ron married and moved to Texas for him to attend Dallas Theological Seminary. They stayed in Texas where Ron led a wilderness camping ministry for troubled youth for many years. Ron now helps corporations with their challenging employees and is the author of the top-rated business book, *No Jerks on the Job*.

Melanie jumped into raising three Texas-born children and serving in ministry to women at her church. Through the years, the Lord has given her opportunity to do Bible teaching and to write grace-based Bible studies for women that are now available from her website (melanienewton.com) and on Bible.org. *Graceful Beginnings* books are for anyone new to the Bible. *Joyful Walk Bible Studies* are for maturing Christians.

Melanie Newton loves to help women learn how to study the Bible for themselves. She also teaches online courses for women to grow their Bible-teaching skills to help others—all with the goal of getting to know Jesus more along the way. Her heart's desire is to encourage you to have a joyful relationship with Jesus Christ so you are willing to share that experience with others around you.

"Jesus took hold of me in 1972, and I've been on this great adventure ever since. My life is a gift of God, full of blessings in the midst of difficult challenges. The more I've learned and experienced God's absolutely amazing grace, the more I've discovered my faith walk to be a joyful one. I'm still seeking that joyful walk every day..."

Melanie

OTHER BIBLE STUDIES BY MELANIE NEWTON

Graceful Beginnings Series books for anyone new to the Bible:

A Fresh Start (basics for new Christians)
Painting the Portrait of Jesus (the Gospel of John)
The God You Can Know (the character of God)
Grace Overflowing (an overview of Paul's 13 letters)
The Walk from Fear to Faith (7 Old Testament women)
Satisfied by His Love (women who knew Jesus)
Seek the Treasure (study of Ephesians)
Pathways to a Joyful Walk (6 pathways to a joy-filled life)

Joyful Walk Bible Studies for growing Christians:

Adorn Yourself with Godliness (1 Timothy and Titus, also in Spanish)
Everyday Women, Ever Faithful God (Old Testament women, also in Spanish)
Connecting Faith to Life on Planet Earth (Genesis 1-11; Revelation)
Graceful Living (the essentials for a grace-based Christian life)
Graceful Living Today (a devotional journal for a joyful life)
Healthy Living (Colossians and Philemon)
Heartbreak to Hope (the Gospel of Mark)
Identity: Sticking to Your Faith in a Pull-Apart World (Ezra thru Malachi)
Knowing Jesus, Knowing Joy (Philippians, also in Spanish)
Live Out His Love (New Testament women)
Perspective (1and 2 Thessalonians)
Profiles of Perseverance (Old Testament men, also in Spanish)
Radical Acts (Acts)
Reboot, Renew, Rejoice (1 and 2 Chronicles)
The God-Dependent Woman (2 Corinthians)
To Be Found Faithful (2 Timothy)

Resources for Leading Others

Be a Christ-Focused Small Group Leader
Leap into Lifestyle Disciplemaking
Bible Study Leadership Made Easy (online video course)
Painting the Picture of Jesus (the "I Am's" of Jesus lessons for children)
Teaching Children the God They Can Know (the character of God for children)

Download our catalogue and get resources for your spiritual growth at melanienewton.com.

CONTENTS

Using This Study Guide

This study guide consists of 11 lessons covering two letters written by the Apostle Paul—1 Timothy and Titus. The lessons are divided into 5 sections (about 25 minutes in length). The first 4 sections contain a detail study of the passages. The fifth section is a podcast that provides additional insight to the lesson.

If you cannot do the entire lesson one week, please read the Bible passage covered by the lesson and try to do the "Day One Study" of the lesson.

THE BASIC STUDY

Each lesson includes core questions covering the passage narrative. These core questions will take you through the process of inductive Bible study—observation, interpretation, and application. It is the best approach for doing Bible Study. The process is more easily understood in the context of answering these questions:

- What does the passage say? *(Observation: what's actually there)*

- What does it mean? *(Interpretation: the author's intended meaning)*

- How does this apply to me today? *(Application: making it personal)*

STUDY ENHANCEMENTS

Deeper Discoveries: Embedded within the sections are *optional* questions for research of subjects we don't have time to cover adequately in the lessons or contain information that significantly enhance the basic study. If you are meeting with a small group, your leader may give you the opportunity to share your "discoveries."

Study Aids: To aid in proper interpretation and application of the study, five additional study aids are located where appropriate in the lesson:

- Historical Insights

- Scriptural Insights

- From the Greek (definitions of Greek words)

- Focus on the Meaning

- Think About It (thoughtful reflection)

- Dependent Living (illustrating what it means to live dependently on God)

Other useful study tools: Use online tools or apps (blueletterbible.org or "Blue Letter Bible app" is especially helpful) to find *cross references* (verses with similar content to what you are studying) and meanings of the *original Greek words or phrases* used (usually called "interlinear"). You can also look at any verse in *various Bible translations* to help with understanding what it is saying.

PODCASTS

Find podcasts for these lessons at melanienewton.com/podcasts (choose "14: 1 Timothy/Titus) and on most podcast providers. Or you can read the blogs associated with the podcasts at melanienewton.com/blog. Choose 1 Timothy / Titus category then scroll to find the title you want. Listen to the first podcast as an introduction to the study.

New Testament Summary

The New Testament opens with the births of John and Jesus. About 30 years later, John challenged the Jews to indicate their repentance (turning from sin and toward God) by submitting to water baptism—a familiar Old Testament practice used for repentance as well as when a Gentile converted to Judaism (to be washed clean of idolatry).

Jesus, God's incarnate Son, publicly showed the world what God is like and taught His perfect ways for 3 – 3½ years. After preparing 12 disciples to continue Christ's earthly work, He died voluntarily on a cross for mankind's sin, rose from the dead, and returned to heaven. The account of His earthly life is recorded in 4 books known as the Gospels (the biblical books of Matthew, Mark, Luke and John named after the compiler of each account).

After Jesus' return to heaven, the followers of Christ were then empowered by the Holy Spirit and spread God's salvation message among the Jews, a number of whom believed in Christ. The apostle Paul and others carried the good news to the Gentiles during 3 missionary journeys (much of this recorded in the book of Acts). Paul wrote 13 New Testament letters to churches & individuals (Romans through Philemon). The section in our Bible from Hebrews to Jude contains 8 additional letters penned by five men, including two apostles (Peter and John) and two of Jesus' half-brothers (James and Jude). The author of Hebrews is unknown. The apostle John also recorded Revelation, which summarizes God's final program for the world. The Bible ends as it began—with a new, sinless creation.

Discussion Group Guidelines

Anyone can do this study alone. If you are doing this as part of a group, we suggest you use the following guidelines to maintain a safe environment for your group members to learn together.

1. **Attend consistently** whether your lesson is done or not. You'll learn from the other women, and they want to get to know you.

2. **Set aside time** to work through the study questions. The goal of Bible study is to **get to know** Jesus. He will change your life.

3. **Share your insights** from your personal study time. As you spend time in the Bible, Jesus will teach you truth through His Spirit inside you.

4. **Respect each other's insights**. Listen thoughtfully. Encourage each other as you interact. Refrain from dominating the discussion if you have a tendency to be talkative. ☺

5. **Celebrate our unity** in Christ. Avoid bringing up controversial subjects such as politics, divisive issues, and denominational differences.

6. **Maintain confidentiality.** Remember that anything shared during the group time is not to leave the **group** (unless permission is granted by the one sharing).

7. **Pray for one another** as sisters in Christ.

8. **Get to know the women** in your group. Please do not use your small group members for solicitation purposes for home businesses, though.

There is a Small Group Discussion Guide located at the end of this book. Anyone can use the guide to lead a group through a discussion of the questions in this study. This is especially useful for groups that have less than two hours to meet together.

Enjoy your Joyful Walk Bible Study!

Paul's First Letter to Timothy (NIV 2011)

Paul, an apostle of Christ Jesus by the command of God our Savior and of Christ Jesus our hope,

To Timothy my true son in the faith:

Grace, mercy and peace from God the Father and Christ Jesus our Lord.

As I urged you when I went into Macedonia, stay there in Ephesus so that you may command certain people not to teach false doctrines any longer or to devote themselves to myths and endless genealogies. Such things promote controversial speculations rather than advancing God's work—which is by faith. The goal of this command is love, which comes from a pure heart and a good conscience and a sincere faith. Some have departed from these and have turned to meaningless talk. They want to be teachers of the law, but they do not know what they are talking about or what they so confidently affirm.

We know that the law is good if one uses it properly. We also know that the law is made not for the righteous but for lawbreakers and rebels, the ungodly and sinful, the unholy and irreligious, for those who kill their fathers or mothers, for murderers, for the sexually immoral, for those practicing homosexuality, for slave traders and liars and perjurers—and for whatever else is contrary to the sound doctrine that conforms to the gospel concerning the glory of the blessed God, which he entrusted to me.

I thank Christ Jesus our Lord, who has given me strength, that he considered me trustworthy, appointing me to his service. Even though I was once a blasphemer and a persecutor and a violent man, I was shown mercy because I acted in ignorance and unbelief. The grace of our Lord was poured out on me abundantly, along with the faith and love that are in Christ Jesus.

Here is a trustworthy saying that deserves full acceptance: Christ Jesus came into the world to save sinners—of whom I am the worst. But for that very reason I was shown mercy so that in me, the worst of sinners, Christ Jesus might display his immense patience as an example for those who would believe in him and receive eternal life. Now to the King eternal, immortal, invisible, the only God, be honor and glory for ever and ever. Amen.

Timothy, my son, I am giving you this command in keeping with the prophecies once made about you, so that by recalling them you may fight the battle well, holding on to faith and a good conscience, which some have rejected and so have suffered shipwreck with regard to the faith. Among them are Hymenaeus and Alexander, whom I have handed over to Satan to be taught not to blaspheme.

I urge, then, first of all, that petitions, prayers, intercession and thanksgiving be made for all people— for kings and all those in authority, that we may live peaceful and quiet lives in all godliness and holiness. This is good, and pleases God our Savior, who wants all people to be saved and to come to a knowledge of the truth. For there is one God and one mediator between God and mankind, the man Christ Jesus, who gave himself as a ransom for all people. This has now been witnessed to at the proper time. And for this purpose I was appointed a herald and an apostle—I am telling the truth, I am not lying—and a true and faithful teacher of the Gentiles.

Therefore I want the men everywhere to pray, lifting up holy hands without anger or disputing. I also want the women to dress modestly, with decency and propriety, adorning themselves, not with elaborate hairstyles or gold or pearls or expensive clothes, but with good deeds, appropriate for women who profess to worship God.

A woman should learn in quietness and full submission. I do not permit a woman to teach or to assume authority over a man; she must be quiet. For Adam was formed first, then Eve. And Adam was not the one deceived; it was the woman who was deceived and became a sinner. But women will be saved through childbearing—if they continue in faith, love and holiness with propriety.

Here is a trustworthy saying: Whoever aspires to be an overseer desires a noble task. Now the overseer is to be above reproach, faithful to his wife, temperate, self-controlled, respectable, hospitable, able to teach, not given to drunkenness, not violent but gentle, not quarrelsome, not a lover of money. He must manage his own family well and see that his children obey him, and he must do so in a manner worthy of full respect. (If anyone does not know how to manage his own family, how can he take care of God's church?) He must not be a recent convert, or he may become conceited and fall under the same judgment as the devil. He must also have a good reputation with outsiders, so that he will not fall into disgrace and into the devil's trap.

In the same way, deacons are to be worthy of respect, sincere, not indulging in much wine, and not pursuing dishonest gain. They must keep hold of the deep truths of the faith with a clear conscience. They must first be tested; and then if there is nothing against them, let them serve as deacons.

In the same way, the women are to be worthy of respect, not malicious talkers but temperate and trustworthy in everything.

A deacon must be faithful to his wife and must manage his children and his household well. Those who have served well gain an excellent standing and great assurance in their faith in Christ Jesus.

Although I hope to come to you soon, I am writing you these instructions so that, if I am delayed, you will know how people ought to conduct themselves in God's household, which is the church of the living God, the pillar and foundation of the truth. Beyond all question, the mystery from which true godliness springs is great:

He appeared in the flesh, was vindicated by the Spirit, was seen by angels, was preached among the nations, was believed on in the world, was taken up in glory.

The Spirit clearly says that in later times some will abandon the faith and follow deceiving spirits and things taught by demons. Such teachings come through hypocritical liars, whose consciences have been seared as with a hot iron. They forbid people to marry and order them to abstain from certain foods, which God created to be received with thanksgiving by those who believe and who know the truth. For everything God created is good, and nothing is to be rejected if it is received with thanksgiving, because it is consecrated by the word of God and prayer.

If you point these things out to the brothers and sisters, you will be a good minister of Christ Jesus, nourished on the truths of the faith and of the good teaching that you have followed. Have nothing to do with godless myths and old wives' tales; rather, train yourself to be godly. For physical training is of some value, but godliness has value for all things, holding promise for both the present life and the life to come. This is a trustworthy saying that deserves full acceptance. That is why we labor and strive, because we have put our hope in the living God, who is the Savior of all people, and especially of those who believe.

Command and teach these things. Don't let anyone look down on you because you are young, but set an example for the believers in speech, in conduct, in love, in faith and in purity. Until I come, devote yourself to the public reading of Scripture, to preaching and to teaching. Do not neglect your gift, which was given you through prophecy when the body of elders laid their hands on you.

Be diligent in these matters; give yourself wholly to them, so that everyone may see your progress. Watch your life and doctrine closely. Persevere in them, because if you do, you will save both yourself and your hearers.

Do not rebuke an older man harshly, but exhort him as if he were your father. Treat younger men as brothers, older women as mothers, and younger women as sisters, with absolute purity.

Give proper recognition to those widows who are really in need. But if a widow has children or grandchildren, these should learn first of all to put their religion into practice by caring for their own family and so repaying their parents and grandparents, for this is pleasing to God. The widow who is really in need and left all alone puts her hope in God and continues night and day to pray and to ask God for help. But the widow who lives for pleasure is dead even while she lives. Give the people these instructions, so that no one may be open to blame. Anyone who does not provide for their relatives, and especially for their own household, has denied the faith and is worse than an unbeliever.

No widow may be put on the list of widows unless she is over sixty, has been faithful to her husband, and is well known for her good deeds, such as bringing up children, showing hospitality, washing the feet of the Lord's people, helping those in trouble and devoting herself to all kinds of good deeds.

As for younger widows, do not put them on such a list. For when their sensual desires overcome their dedication to Christ, they want to marry. Thus they bring judgment on themselves, because they have broken their first pledge. Besides, they get into the habit of being idle and going about from house to house. And not only do they become idlers, but also busybodies who talk nonsense, saying things they ought not to. So I counsel younger widows to marry, to have children, to manage their homes and to give the enemy no opportunity for slander. Some have in fact already turned away to follow Satan.

If any woman who is a believer has widows in her care, she should continue to help them and not let the church be burdened with them, so that the church can help those widows who are really in need.

The elders who direct the affairs of the church well are worthy of double honor, especially those whose work is preaching and teaching. For Scripture says, "Do not muzzle an ox while it is treading out the grain," and "The worker deserves his wages." Do not entertain an accusation against an elder unless it is brought by two or three witnesses. But those elders who are sinning you are to reprove before everyone, so that the others may take warning. I charge you, in the sight of God and Christ Jesus and the elect angels, to keep these instructions without partiality, and to do nothing out of favoritism.

Do not be hasty in the laying on of hands, and do not share in the sins of others. Keep yourself pure.

Stop drinking only water, and use a little wine because of your stomach and your frequent illnesses.

The sins of some are obvious, reaching the place of judgment ahead of them; the sins of others trail behind them. In the same way, good deeds are obvious, and even those that are not obvious cannot remain hidden forever.

All who are under the yoke of slavery should consider their masters worthy of full respect, so that God's name and our teaching may not be slandered. Those who have believing masters should not show them disrespect just because they are fellow believers. Instead, they should serve them even better because their masters are dear to them as fellow believers and are devoted to the welfare of their slaves.

These are the things you are to teach and insist on. If anyone teaches otherwise and does not agree to the sound instruction of our Lord Jesus Christ and to godly teaching, they are conceited and understand nothing. They have an unhealthy interest in controversies and quarrels about words that result in envy, strife, malicious talk, evil suspicions and constant friction between people of corrupt mind, who have been robbed of the truth and who think that godliness is a means to financial gain.

But godliness with contentment is great gain. For we brought nothing into the world, and we can take nothing out of it. But if we have food and clothing, we will be content with that. Those who want to get rich fall into temptation and a trap and into many foolish and harmful desires that plunge people into ruin and destruction. For the love of money is a root of all kinds of evil. Some people, eager for money, have wandered from the faith and pierced themselves with many griefs.

But you, man of God, flee from all this, and pursue righteousness, godliness, faith, love, endurance and gentleness. Fight the good fight of the faith. Take hold of the eternal life to which you were called when you made your good confession in the presence of many witnesses. In the sight of God, who gives life to everything, and of Christ Jesus, who while testifying before Pontius Pilate made the good confession, I charge you to keep this command without spot or blame until the appearing of our Lord Jesus Christ, which God will bring about in his own time—God, the blessed and only Ruler, the King of kings and Lord of lords, who alone is immortal and who lives in unapproachable light, whom no one has seen or can see. To him be honor and might forever. Amen.

Command those who are rich in this present world not to be arrogant nor to put their hope in wealth, which is so uncertain, but to put their hope in God, who richly provides us with everything for our enjoyment. Command them to do good, to be rich in good deeds, and to be generous and willing to share. In this way they will lay up treasure for themselves as a firm foundation for the coming age, so that they may take hold of the life that is truly life.

Timothy, guard what has been entrusted to your care. Turn away from godless chatter and the opposing ideas of what is falsely called knowledge, which some have professed and in so doing have departed from the faith.

Grace be with you all.

Paul's Letter to Titus (NIV 2011)

Paul, a servant of God and an apostle of Jesus Christ to further the faith of God's elect and their knowledge of the truth that leads to godliness— in the hope of eternal life, which God, who does not lie, promised before the beginning of time, and which now at his appointed season he has brought to light through the preaching entrusted to me by the command of God our Savior,

To Titus, my true son in our common faith:

Grace and peace from God the Father and Christ Jesus our Savior.

The reason I left you in Crete was that you might put in order what was left unfinished and appoint elders in every town, as I directed you. An elder must be blameless, faithful to his wife, a man whose children believe and are not open to the charge of being wild and disobedient. Since an overseer manages God's household, he must be blameless—not overbearing, not quick-tempered, not given to drunkenness, not violent, not pursuing dishonest gain. Rather, he must be hospitable, one who loves what is good, who is self-controlled, upright, holy and disciplined. He must hold firmly to the trustworthy message as it has been taught, so that he can encourage others by sound doctrine and refute those who oppose it.

 For there are many rebellious people, full of meaningless talk and deception, especially those of the circumcision group. They must be silenced, because they are disrupting whole households by teaching things they ought not to teach—and that for the sake of dishonest gain. One of Crete's own prophets has said it: "Cretans are always liars, evil brutes, lazy gluttons." This saying is true. Therefore rebuke them sharply, so that they will be sound in the faith and will pay no attention to Jewish myths or to the merely human commands of those who reject the truth. To the pure, all things are pure, but to those who are corrupted and do not believe, nothing is pure. In fact, both their minds and consciences are corrupted. They claim to know God, but by their actions they deny him. They are detestable, disobedient and unfit for doing anything good.

You, however, must teach what is appropriate to sound doctrine. Teach the older men to be temperate, worthy of respect, self-controlled, and sound in faith, in love and in endurance.

Likewise, teach the older women to be reverent in the way they live, not to be slanderers or addicted to much wine, but to teach what is good. Then they can urge the younger women to love their husbands and children, to be self-controlled and pure, to be busy at home, to be kind, and to be subject to their husbands, so that no one will malign the word of God.

Similarly, encourage the young men to be self-controlled. In everything set them an example by doing what is good. In your teaching show integrity, seriousness and soundness of speech that cannot be condemned, so that those who oppose you may be ashamed because they have nothing bad to say about us.

Teach slaves to be subject to their masters in everything, to try to please them, not to talk back to them, and not to steal from them, but to show that they can be fully trusted, so that in every way they will make the teaching about God our Savior attractive.

For the grace of God has appeared that offers salvation to all people. It teaches us to say "No" to ungodliness and worldly passions, and to live self-controlled, upright and godly lives in this present age, while we wait for the blessed hope—the appearing of the glory of our great God and Savior, Jesus Christ, who gave himself for us to redeem us from all wickedness and to purify for himself a people that are his very own, eager to do what is good.

These, then, are the things you should teach. Encourage and rebuke with all authority. Do not let anyone despise you.

Remind the people to be subject to rulers and authorities, to be obedient, to be ready to do whatever is good, to slander no one, to be peaceable and considerate, and always to be gentle toward everyone.

At one time we too were foolish, disobedient, deceived and enslaved by all kinds of passions and pleasures. We lived in malice and envy, being hated and hating one another. But when the kindness and love of God our Savior appeared, he saved us, not because of righteous things we had done, but because of his mercy. He saved us through the washing of rebirth and renewal by the Holy Spirit, whom he poured out on us generously through Jesus Christ our Savior, so that, having been justified by his grace, we might become heirs having the hope of eternal life. This is a trustworthy saying. And I want you to stress these things, so that those who have trusted in God may be careful to devote themselves to doing what is good. These things are excellent and profitable for everyone.

But avoid foolish controversies and genealogies and arguments and quarrels about the law, because these are unprofitable and useless. Warn a divisive person once, and then warn them a second time. After that, have nothing to do with them. You may be sure that such people are warped and sinful; they are self-condemned.

As soon as I send Artemas or Tychicus to you, do your best to come to me at Nicopolis, because I have decided to winter there. Do everything you can to help Zenas the lawyer and Apollos on their way and see that they have everything they need. Our people must learn to devote themselves to doing what is good, in order to provide for urgent needs and not live unproductive lives.

Everyone with me sends you greetings. Greet those who love us in the faith.

Grace be with you all.

Recommended: Listen to the podcast "The What and Why of Godliness" as an introduction to the whole study. Use the following listener guide.

The What and Why of Godliness

Every morning when you approach the mirror to get ready, do you wish that you could simply put on one thing, or do just one thing, that would present you to the world looking just the way you would like to look? You can do that! Each and every day, you can adorn yourself with godliness.

WHAT "ADORN YOURSELF" MEANS

- The English word "adorn" translates the Greek word *kosmeo* from which we get our word "cosmetic." It means, "to arrange, to put in order, make ready, to ornament." We adorn ourselves in daily life to fulfill a purpose. Adorning yourself is a good thing.

WHAT GODLINESS MEANS

Godliness is devotion to God expressed in a life that is pleasing to Him.

- Devotion to God means you are dedicated to Him. You are firmly attached to Him. Whatever He wants, you want. It is a loyal love for God.

- Godliness is devotion in action. Your loyal love for God expresses itself in a life that reflects His character. Who He is. And that is pleasing to Him.

- We adorn ourselves with godliness by first being completely devoted to Him, loving Him so much that we want to reflect His character as we live our lives. We take on His likeness—Godlikeness, not becoming God but presenting Him.

- Jesus is our example of godliness as a human. He presented the attributes of Father God to everyone who saw Him. He adorned Himself with godliness through humility, compassion, love, prayer, dependency on God the Father, good works, and many more ways. His devotion to God was expressed in a life that reflected God and was pleasing to God. *John 14:6*

- Devotion to God is not just living by a set of rules. God isn't interested in outward conformity. When our hearts are right, we will want to obey Him with our thinking and behavior. We will want to reflect Him well because we love Him so much.

ADORNING OURSELVES WITH CHRIST

- Since Jesus is our example of what it looks like to adorn ourselves with godliness, we need to read through the Gospels, getting to know Jesus well. Then, we should continue reading through the whole New Testament to get the big picture of how those early Christians adorned themselves with godliness. We can learn from their examples.

- The absolutely wonderful news is this: We have been given everything we need for godliness. First, through knowing Him. Then, we get His divine power. The Holy Spirit begins to work right away at transforming you to look more like Christ. *2 Peter 1:3*

- From the time you are saved until you die and enter heaven, you are never without the ability to be godly. It's not based on your own ability but on His power working to bring about godliness in you. We CAN live a godly life because of His Spirit in us.

- But, it's a cooperative effort. He is always working. But, we can resist His work. That's why godliness begins with devotion to God—loving Him so much that you want to live a godly life that pleases Him.

- It's not perfection. It's loyal love for God that leads to obedience and humility and awareness of Whose we are and why we are here.

WHY SHOULD CHRISTIAN WOMEN DESIRE TO ADORN OURSELVES WITH GODLINESS?

- You and I should desire to adorn ourselves with godliness …

  - ✓ **For God the Father and our Lord Jesus Christ** because of our love for them and gratitude for what they have done for our salvation (1 Timothy 4:10). This is our first and foremost reason.

  - ✓ **For ourselves and our fellow Christians** because godly behavior is good for us in every way (1 Timothy 6:6, 19; Titus 2:11-13).

  - ✓ **For others who are watching us** because godliness makes the teaching about Christ attractive and draws unbelievers to the God we know and serve (Titus 2:10).

- Among those watching are the "fashion police"—the ones who oppose Christ and the Gospel, looking for an excuse not to believe. When we adorn ourselves with godliness, there is nothing for "them" to accuse.

- Among those watching are the "shoppers"—with hearts open to God. They just need to see Him through you and I displaying His character. They want to believe.

- For anyone watching, when we adorn ourselves with godliness because of our love for Him, the word of God will not be dishonored or discredited.

YOU CAN MAKE THE DAILY CHOICE TO ADORN YOURSELF WITH GODLINESS.

Every morning, as you look in the mirror, see **who you really are**, a woman of God who is totally loved and accepted by Him because of your faith in His Son Jesus Christ. What could be a more beautiful, worthwhile goal than to adorn yourself with godliness … to put yourself in order with the very character of God … to arrange to live your life properly displaying the beliefs you profess … to dress, act, and be like Him for Him!

Let Jesus satisfy your heart with such love for God that you will want to live a life that pleases Him.

1: Introduction to 1 Timothy and Titus

DAY ONE STUDY

Ask the Lord Jesus to teach you through His Word.

The ABCs of 1 Timothy and Titus—Author, Background, and Context

Like any book you read, it always helps to know a bit about the author, the background setting for the story (i.e., past, present, future), and where the book fits into a series (that's the context). The same is true of Bible books.

AUTHOR

The apostle Paul identifies himself as the author of the letters written to Timothy and to Titus. Paul, whose Hebrew name was Saul, was born in Tarsus, a major Roman city on the coast of southeast Asia Minor. Tarsus was the center for the tent making industry. Paul was trained in that craft as his occupation (his primary paying profession). As a Jewish Pharisee from the tribe of Benjamin, Paul was educated at the feet of Gamaliel, a well-respected rabbi of the day. Paul was an ardent persecutor of the early church until his life-changing conversion to Christianity

After believing in Jesus Christ as his Savior, Paul was sent by God as an apostle to take the gospel to the Gentiles. This was an amazing about-face for a committed Pharisee like Paul who ordinarily would have nothing to do with Gentiles. Paul wrote 13 letters that are included in the New Testament. Tradition has it that Paul was beheaded shortly after he wrote 2 Timothy in 67 A.D. *(You can glean more about Paul's background from Acts 8:3; 9:1-31; 22:3-5; 26:9-11; and Galatians 1:11-24.)*

BACKGROUND

During Paul's first two missionary journeys, he traveled through central Turkey, establishing several churches in that area, including Lystra. Timothy first heard Paul preach the gospel on Paul's first visit to Lystra and trusted in Christ, likely as a teen. His mother, Eunice, and grandmother, Lois, were devout Jews who became believers in Christ. Timothy's father was a Greek. We know nothing more about him. Paul became Timothy's spiritual father. Timothy may have seen Paul heal a lame man in his town. He may have watched the angry mob throw stones at Paul and leave him for dead (Acts 14:8-20). Yet, he also knew Paul survived. When Paul came back to Lystra a couple of years later on his second journey, Paul invited Timothy to travel with him. During that time, Timothy helped to establish churches at Philippi, Thessalonica, and Corinth. Six of Paul's letters to churches include Timothy in the salutations meaning Timothy was with him when Paul wrote the letters.

Like Timothy, Titus responded with faith in Christ as he heard Paul preach about Jesus in Antioch (Syria). Paul brought Titus as a Gentile (non-Jewish) Christian to Jerusalem to show the apostles and other Jewish believers how a Gentile was completely accepted by God through faith in Jesus Christ through the gospel.

During the 3 years Paul was teaching in Ephesus (his third missionary journey), both Timothy and Titus were there with him. Then, Paul sent Titus to Corinth to alleviate tension at that church and to collect money for the poor. Like Timothy, Paul thought of Titus as his spiritual son because he had led him to trust Christ.

At the end of Paul's third missionary journey, he traveled to Jerusalem in the spring of 57 A.D. to deliver an offering collected by the Gentile churches to help the impoverished Jewish Christians.

After being accused by the Jews of some technical violation of the Jewish Law, Paul was arrested by the Romans and spent the next two years in Caesarea as a prisoner. Paul appealed to Caesar so he was sent to Rome. There he lived under house arrest for another two years. Timothy was with him during that time.

After Paul's release from this first Roman imprisonment (around 62 A.D.), he and Timothy traveled to Ephesus. Paul discovered that during his absence, the church was plagued with all kinds of spiritual problems. The city of Ephesus, with all of its corruption and idolatry, was proving to be a spiritual battleground for the congregation of believers meeting in house churches there. As Paul moved on to Macedonia, he left Timothy in Ephesus to care for the church. Paul wrote 1 Timothy around 64 A.D. from Rome or Macedonia to encourage Timothy in his work.

While Timothy was in Ephesus, Paul and Titus traveled to the island of Crete to share the gospel and establish churches. Paul wanted to go visit the church in Corinth so he left Titus in Crete to continue teaching the new Christians and to appoint church leaders for each new church. Paul wrote the letter to Titus (around 65 A.D.) soon after writing 1 Timothy, probably while Paul was in Macedonia, on his way to Nicopolis (northwestern Greece). Titus rejoined Paul in western Macedonia and continued his missionary work northward into Dalmatia (now Albania).

CONTEXT

In our New Testaments, we have nine letters of Paul written to churches (Romans, 1 and 2 Corinthians, Galatians, Ephesians, Philippians, Colossians, and 1 and 2 Thessalonians). We also have four of Paul's letters written to individuals (1 and 2 Timothy, Titus, and Philemon). Ephesians, Philippians, Colossians, and Philemon were written during Paul's Roman house arrest. The letters called 1 Timothy and Titus were written a couple of years after his release. Paul wrote 2 Timothy later as he waited in a Roman dungeon for his certain execution.

Paul's three letters—1 Timothy, 2 Timothy, and Titus—are called "pastoral epistles" because for the most part they are Paul's counsel to his representatives to the local churches in the regions of Ephesus and Crete. The three letters address the issues facing local churches—by the pastoral leaders as well as the members.

1. What grabbed your attention from the ABCs above?

Adorn Yourself with Godliness

What comes to mind when you hear the phrase, "adorn yourself?" The English word "adorn" translates the Greek word *kosmeo* from which we get our word "cosmetic." It means, "to arrange, to put in order, make ready, to ornament." That's what women do when we style our hair, put on makeup, and dress ourselves.

Have you ever thought that as you were applying your make-up, you were actually putting your face in order? When you get ready for a big job interview, you're actually arranging yourself in such a way by what you wear and how you act to demonstrate that you are truly the right person for the job. And, if you are married, you might make arrangements for a special dinner with your spouse and adorn yourself with his favorite dress, hairstyle and perfume. We adorn our homes to reflect who we are. We adorn ourselves in daily life to fulfill a purpose. Adorning yourself is a good thing.

"Adorn" is also an important word in the Bible. That Greek word *kosmeo* is used 12 times in the original language of the New Testament. In Luke 21:5, the disciples remarked to Jesus about how the temple was adorned with beautiful stones and with gifts dedicated to God. In Revelation 21:2,19, the apostle John described his vision of the new Jerusalem coming down out of heaven from God, "prepared as a bride beautifully dressed for her husband," adorned "with every kind of precious stone." And, it is used three times (1 Timothy 2:9; Titus 2:10; and 1 Peter 3:5) about believers adorning themselves in such a way as to please the Lord and make the gospel attractive to nonbelievers. Adorning fulfills a purpose. We are to adorn ourselves with something called godliness.

So, what does it mean to adorn yourself with godliness?

Godliness (from the Greek *eusebeia*) conveys the idea of a personal attitude toward God that results in actions that are pleasing to Him. This personal attitude toward God is devotion to God. But, it's not just a warm, emotional feeling about God that we get when we have private Bible reading and prayer or sing worship songs. It is always devotion in action. Something results from our devotion.

True devotion to God always results in godly character. Your love for God expresses itself in a life that is pleasing to God. So, godliness can be defined as **devotion to God expressed in a life that is pleasing to Him.**

We adorn ourselves with godliness by first being completely devoted to Him, loving Him so much that we want to reflect His character as we live our lives. We take on His likeness—Godlikeness, not becoming God but presenting Him. Attributes of godliness are those same ones found in our Lord Jesus—humility, compassion, love, prayer, dependency on God the Father, and many more.

God isn't interested in outward conformity. He doesn't just want us to act properly. He's interested in our hearts first. When our hearts are right, we will want to obey Him with our thinking and behavior. We will want to reflect Him well because we love Him so much. Godliness begins in the heart and mind then is lived out in words and behavior.

We adorn ourselves with godliness for God the Father and Jesus Christ because of our love for them and gratitude for what they have done for our salvation (1 Timothy 4:10). We adorn ourselves with godliness for ourselves and our fellow Christians because godly behavior is good for us in every way (1 Timothy 6:6, 19; Titus 2:11-13). And, adorning ourselves with godliness makes the teaching about Christ attractive, drawing unbelievers to the God we know and serve (Titus 2:10).

What could be a more beautiful, worthwhile goal than to adorn yourself with godliness…to put yourself in order with the very character of God … to arrange or live your life properly displaying the beliefs you claim to profess … to dress, act, and be like Him for Him! That is our hope for each of you as you learn from God's Word through Paul's letters to Timothy and Titus.

2. What grabbed your attention from this introduction to adorning yourself with godliness?

Respond to the Lord about what you learned today.

DAY TWO STUDY—GET THE BIG PICTURE OF 1 TIMOTHY AND TITUS

Ask the Lord Jesus to teach you through His Word.

In all of our *Joyful Walk Bible Studies*, we follow the inductive process for Bible Study. The inductive process starts with observation, looking carefully at what the text actually says. ***What does the Bible say?*** The next step is interpretation, which is trying to understand the author's intended meaning—to him and to the audience who would read or hear it. ***What does it mean?*** Once you know what the Bible says and what it means, then you are ready for application, which is learning how to live this out in your life. ***What application will you make?*** When you follow the inductive process for Bible Study, you will be able to confidently dwell in that truth.

What does the Bible say? (This is the "Observation" step in the process of Bible Study.)

Where do we begin? Have you ever heard the saying: "You can't see the forest for the trees?" The best way to study any book of the Bible is to begin with the "forest" (survey the whole) and then proceed to the "trees" (the individual parts). We will start by getting an overview of what Paul wrote in both letters. Several common themes are woven throughout Paul's instruction to Timothy and Titus. We will read them both as they were intended—letters from one dear friend to another. Ready to get started? Let's go!

Today, read the letter called *1 Timothy* at one sitting. It will take about 15 minutes. You can read the letter in any translation of the Bible you choose. A copy of 1 Timothy (NIV translation) is included in this study guide before Lesson One. Feel free to mark anything that grabs your attention. Then, answer the questions below.

3. What do you remember most from your reading of this letter?

4. What were the main subjects that Paul covered in this letter?

5. After reading this letter, do you have a better understanding of what godliness looks like in contrast to that which is ungodly?

6. What questions do you have after reading 1 Timothy that you would like to have answered in this study?

> **Scriptural Insight:** This letter of Paul's has more references to women than any other one. There are some verses that are difficult to understand and may remain a mystery until we get to heaven. But, there is plenty of truth revealed for us to know and apply in our lives on earth now. We will dwell in truth we can know and must humbly accept that which we don't know or understand. ☺

Ask the Lord to show you what He wants you to learn through this study of 1 Timothy.

DAY THREE STUDY

Ask the Lord Jesus to teach you through His Word.

What does the Bible say? (This is the "Observation" step in the process of Bible Study.)

Today, read the letter called *Titus* at one sitting. It will take about 7 minutes. You can read the letter in any translation of the Bible you choose. A copy of Titus (NIV translation) is included in this study guide before Lesson One. Feel free to mark anything that grabs your attention. Then, answer the questions below.

7. What do you remember most from your reading of this letter?

8. What subjects did you see in this letter that you also read in 1 Timothy?

9. After reading this letter, do you have a better understanding of what godliness looks like in contrast to that which is ungodly?

10. What questions do you have after reading Titus that you would like to have answered in this study?

Ask the Lord to show you what He wants you to learn through this study of Titus.

DAY FOUR STUDY

Ask the Lord Jesus to teach you through His Word.

What does it mean? (This is the "Interpretation" step in the process of Bible Study.)

Remember that our definition of godliness is **"devotion to God expressed in a life that is pleasing to Him."** Godliness begins in the heart and mind (devotion to God) then is lived out in words and behavior (expressed in a life that is pleasing to Him).

Jesus confirmed in His teaching that devotion to God begins with loving God with all your heart, soul, mind, and strength (Mark 12:30). In order to love God, you need to know Him. Right? In order to be devoted to God the Father and the Lord Jesus Christ, you need to know the truth about them and the truth about the gospel message that is the foundation of your faith. Truth enhances your devotion to God. Error takes you away from your devotion to Him (2 Corinthians 11:3). So, one of the major themes in all of Paul's letters, and especially in the pastoral letters, is this: *teach and maintain truth and sound doctrine while guarding against error.*

TEACH AND MAINTAIN TRUTH AND SOUND DOCTRINE WHILE GUARDING AGAINST ERROR.

What you believe about God and about yourself in relationship to God directs how you think and, therefore, how you act. As you read in Titus 1:1, knowledge of the truth leads to godliness. "Truth and sound doctrine" refer to the truth we get from God's Word and, especially, the truths about the Christian faith (1 Timothy 3:9). You have to know what it is in order to teach and maintain it. This theme really breaks down into positive versus negative aspects.

11. The **Positive**: "teach and maintain truth and sound doctrine."

- Read 1 Timothy 2:3-6 and Titus 3:4-7. What truth about the Christian faith must be upheld?

- Read 1 Timothy 3:9; 4:6, 10-11, 16 and Titus 1:9; 2:1. What is repeatedly emphasized about maintaining truth?

12. The **Negative**: "guard against error."

- Read 1 Timothy 1:3-4 and Titus 1:10-11, 13-16. What can generally happen when we allow those who teach error into our church community?

- Read 1 Timothy 6:20-21 and Titus 1:9; 3:9-10. What are we supposed to do when we encounter error?

Truth leads to godliness (Titus 1:1). So, another major theme of the pastoral letters is this: *adorn yourself with godliness versus ungodliness.*

ADORNING YOURSELF WITH GODLINESS VS. UNGODLINESS

Remember that our definition of godliness is *"devotion to God expressed in a life that is pleasing to Him."* Godliness begins in the heart and mind then is lived out in words and behavior. As you read the two letters, you saw a repeated emphasis on godliness in thought and behavior as the way to please God and impact the world around you.

Scriptural Insight: You may have heard someone say, "Cleanliness is next to godliness." That is not biblical. No amount of disinfecting spray or wipes can cleanse a human heart. God does the cleansing of the heart who puts its trust in Him by faith in Jesus Christ.

13. Let's look at several New Testament verses that include the quality of godliness in them. The translators use "godliness" (noun) and "godly" (adverb, adjective). Godliness and godly all refer to the devotion to God expressed in a life that is pleasing to Him.

    - Read 2 Peter 1:3. What have we been given?

    - Read 2 Peter 1:5. What are we to do?

    - Read 2 Peter 3:11-12. How are we to live and why?

    - Read 1 Timothy 4:7-8 and 1 Timothy 6:11. What action are we to take regarding godliness?

    - Read Titus 2:11-12. What does the grace of God teach us to do?

    - Read Acts 3:12-16. Possessing godliness always points to whom?

    Think About It: The "form" or appearance of godliness may include going to church, knowing Christian doctrine, using Christian clichés, and following a community's Christian traditions. Such practices can make a person look good, but if the inner attitudes of belief, love, and worship are lacking, the outer appearance is meaningless. Paul warns us not to be deceived by people who only appear to be Christians. It may be difficult to distinguish them from true Christians at first, but their daily behavior will give them away. (*The NIV Life Application Study Bible*, note on 2 Timothy 3:5)

14. Read Titus 2:10 (especially the last part) in several translations, including the NASB. What is one of the purposes of pursuing godliness in our lives?

What application will you make to adorn yourself with godliness? (This is the "Application" step in the process of Bible Study.)

15. *Truth versus error:* If Paul made so many comments on the same subject, it should be taken seriously and seen as a pattern woven throughout each letter.

  - What could happen to the local church...therefore you...if we do not seriously apply Paul's message to Timothy, Titus, and the church to stay faithful to God's truth and guard against error?

  - What specific actions can you or do you take in your daily life to ensure that you don't wander away from God's truth and your sincere devotion to God?

16. **Respond to the Lord about what you learned today:** Adorning yourself with godliness will not only benefit yourself but will also benefit everyone around you. Know also that we are never left on our own to try really, really hard to be godly. We have the Holy Spirit inside us who teaches us how to live godly lives. He has the power and the purpose to transform us to look more like Christ than our old self-centered selves. We cooperate by desiring Him to change us and depending on Him to do that in our lives. Will you ask Him today to give you a desire for godliness in your life and to work in those areas where you do not reflect the life of Jesus well?

Respond to the Lord about what you learned today.

Recommended: Listen to the podcast "Grasping God's Truth Is Essential to Godliness" after doing this lesson to reinforce what you have learned. Use the following listener guide.

Grasping God's Truth Is Essential to Godliness

Truth enhances your devotion to God. Error takes you away from Him. Both influence how you adorn yourself. Grasping God's truth is essential to godliness.

TEACH AND MAINTAIN TRUTH; GUARD AGAINST ERROR.

- Any error that persists is like a spiritual infection in the Body of Christ. And, like an infection in the human body, it always affects life so it must be addressed.

- The answer to all spiritual infections is the truth that has been given to us in the Bible, especially in the New Testament. The historical reliability of the Scriptures can be investigated to show that the biblical records are trustworthy.

DWELL IN TRUTH YOU CAN KNOW.

- To dwell in truth is to make your home there. That means God's truth dominates your thoughts and attitudes, governs your life, and satisfies your heart.

- Read through the Gospels, getting to know Jesus well. Then, continue reading through the whole New Testament to get the big picture of what your salvation is all about. Then, go back and read through the Old Testament to get the grand picture of God and His plan throughout the ages.

- God gives us plenty of truth in the Bible that we can know and trust. 66 books, 1189 chapters!

- God wants us to know the truth He has revealed to us, to make our home in that truth.

HUMBLY ACCEPT WHAT YOU DON'T KNOW OR UNDERSTAND.

- Some things we read in the Bible we don't understand now but might in the future. There is much we can know now. But, there are things we'll never know or understand. *Deuteronomy 29:29*

- We can do our best to try to understand what is written. When you run across something that you can't seem to understand from a Bible passage, make the choice to humbly accept what you don't know or understand.

DISCERN ALL TEACHING THROUGH THE COMPLETE REVELATION OF GOD'S WORD.

1. Evaluate what you read and hear by comparing it with the whole Bible.

- Don't let experience and feelings determine your truth.

- Read any verse in the context of the passage where it is found—the paragraph, the chapter, and the book.

- Look at other verses with similar content to let the Bible interpret itself. And, you should always ask the Holy Spirit for understanding.

- Remember that even the best teachers are not infallible. Most are 80-90% right in what they teach and would love to know where they are wrong so they can change it. Always check what you read and hear with what the Word of God says.

2. Avoid the "look-imagine-see dragon" when viewing any verse.

The "look-imagine-see" dragon shows up this way: someone *looks* at a verse or passage, *imagines* what they want it to say, then their mind *sees* what they have imagined through twisting word meanings and interpretations. Once it starts, it's like a fiery dragon burning truth in its path. Cultural influence on Bible study feeds this dragon.

- Tame the "look-imagine-see dragon" by considering the Bible as sufficient on its own, not needing our "improvement."

- Tame the "look-imagine-see dragon" by basing your faith on what **is** in God's Word, not something you've just heard about it and not something you're imagining to be there.

- Tame the "look-imagine-see dragon" by following the inductive process for Bible Study—observation, interpretation, and application. Then, you can confidently dwell in that truth you can know.

CONCLUSION

Grasping God's truth is essential for godliness. Grasping truth protects you and preserves your freedom. Believers in Jesus Christ should never stop learning His word and learning from His word. Everything we go through adds to it as we make the right decisions and learn to avoid the bad ones.

> The Bible is the greatest of all books; to study it is the noblest of all pursuits; to understand it, the highest of all goals. (Charles Ryrie)

Receive the word of God. Accept it not as a human word, but as it actually is, the word of God. Then, let it permeate your whole being so that you will not only be devoted to God but also be able to adorn yourself with godliness.

Let Jesus satisfy your heart with such love for God that you will want to live a life that pleases Him.

2: Dressed in Truth that Strengthens Devotion to God

1 Timothy 1:1-20

DAY ONE STUDY—GET THE BIG PICTURE

What does the Bible say? (This is the "Observation" step of Bible Study.)

Let's start digging into this wonderful letter from God to us—1 Timothy. For every lesson, we will begin with reading the whole passage to get the big picture before we study the verses more closely.

Ask the Lord Jesus to teach you through His Word.

Read the Bible passage below (NIV). Use your own method (colored pencils, lines, shapes) to mark 1) anything that grabs your attention, 2) words you want to understand, and 3) anything repeated in this passage. Draw arrows between thoughts that connect. Put a star ✱ next to anything you think relates to godliness.

1 *Paul, an apostle of Christ Jesus by the command of God our Savior and of Christ Jesus our hope, ² To Timothy my true son in the faith: Grace, mercy and peace from God the Father and Christ Jesus our Lord.*

³ As I urged you when I went into Macedonia, stay there in Ephesus so that you may command certain people not to teach false doctrines any longer ⁴ or to devote themselves to myths and endless genealogies. Such things promote controversial speculations rather than advancing God's work—which is by faith. ⁵ The goal of this command is love, which comes from a pure heart and a good conscience and a sincere faith. ⁶ Some have departed from these and have turned to meaningless talk. ⁷ They want to be teachers of the law, but they do not know what they are talking about or what they so confidently affirm.

⁸ We know that the law is good if one uses it properly. ⁹ We also know that the law is made not for the righteous but for lawbreakers and rebels, the ungodly and sinful, the unholy and irreligious, for those who kill their fathers or mothers, for murderers, ¹⁰ for the sexually immoral, for those practicing homosexuality, for slave traders and liars and perjurers—and for whatever else is contrary to the sound doctrine ¹¹ that conforms to the gospel concerning the glory of the blessed God, which he entrusted to me.

¹² I thank Christ Jesus our Lord, who has given me strength, that he considered me trustworthy, appointing me to his service. ¹³ Even though I was once a blasphemer and a persecutor and a violent man, I was shown mercy because I acted in ignorance and unbelief. ¹⁴ The grace of our Lord was poured out on me abundantly, along with the faith and love that are in Christ Jesus.

¹⁵ Here is a trustworthy saying that deserves full acceptance: Christ Jesus came into the world to save sinners—of whom I am the worst. ¹⁶ But for that very reason I was shown mercy so that in me, the worst of sinners, Christ Jesus might display his immense patience as an example for those who would believe in him and receive eternal life. ¹⁷ Now to the King eternal, immortal, invisible, the only God, be honor and glory for ever and ever. Amen.

¹⁸ Timothy, my son, I am giving you this command in keeping with the prophecies once made about you, so that by recalling them you may fight the battle well, ¹⁹ holding on to faith and a good conscience, which some have rejected and so have suffered shipwreck with regard to the faith. ²⁰ Among them are Hymenaeus and Alexander, whom I have handed over to Satan to be taught not to blaspheme.

1. What grabbed your attention from 1 Timothy 1:1-20?

2. What verses or specific words do you want to understand better?

3. What words or phrases are repeated in this passage? Give verses.

4. What verses illustrate or help you understand what godliness looks like?

5. ***Adorn yourself with godliness:*** From this lesson's passage (1 Timothy 1:1-20), choose one verse to dwell upon all week long. Write it in the space below. Ask God to teach you through this verse.

Respond to the Lord about what He's shown you today.

DAY TWO STUDY

Read 1 Timothy 1:1-20. Ask the Lord Jesus to teach you through His Word.

We will focus on vv. 1-2, 12-17 in this session.

What does it mean?

> **Historical Insight:** The church at Ephesus had been founded about 10 years before this time (Acts 19). Ephesus was a harbor city on the west coast of modern Turkey. Two words described Ephesus—prominent and obsessed. It was prominent as a major commercial center along several trade routes with impressive buildings, a large population of 1/4 million people, and the Roman governor's office. Ephesus was obsessed as a center for spiritualism in the Roman world filled with magicians, psychics, astrologers, and the worship of Artemis, a fertility goddess. For the Ephesians, life was all about who or what had the most power. They thought their magic and their goddess Artemis were powerful enough to satisfy their spiritual needs. Then, Paul introduced them to Jesus. They soon found out that what they had was worthless compared to what Paul offered them. God did extra-miraculous things among them to show off His power. Paul's ministry success threatened the livelihood of local silversmiths who fashioned silver shrines and images of Artemis to sell to the tourist-worshipers. This caused a riot in the city (Acts 19:28-41), endangering the lives of Paul and his ministry team. Timothy was there during the 3 years Paul was teaching in Ephesus. So, he was part of the founding of this church and well-known to its members. By now, Timothy was a young man of about 30 who for 13 years had gained experience at teaching the truth about Jesus and serving God's people well as he watched Paul do it.

6. How does Paul identify himself in v. 1? Why would this be an important truth to include for Timothy as well as anyone else who reads his letter?

7. *Deeper Discoveries (optional):* This letter is addressed to Timothy. To learn more about Timothy, read Acts 16:1-3; 1 Corinthians 4:17; 1 Corinthians 16:10-11; Philippians 2:19-24; 1 Thessalonians 3:2; 1 Timothy 4:12; and Hebrews 13:23. What can we know about Timothy—who he is, his character, and how Paul regarded him?

> **Scriptural Insight:** Six of Paul's epistles include Timothy in the salutations. The most tender and moving of Paul's letters was his last one to Timothy. He was a prisoner in a Roman dungeon when he wrote 2 Timothy, approximately 67 A.D. Paul knew he had a short time to live, so the letter is his spiritual last will and testament to encourage Timothy and to request that Timothy join him during his final days of imprisonment (2 Timothy 1:4, 4:9, 21).

8. Paul usually began his letters with the greeting "grace and peace from God" (1 Timothy 1:2). Grace (Greek, *charis*) was a common greeting among the Greeks, and peace (Hebrew, *shalom*) was a common greeting among Jews. Paul combined them together, elevating their meaning. Read Romans 5:1-2. What is the connection between grace and peace?

Remember that our definition of godliness is *"devotion to God expressed in a life that is pleasing to Him."* Godliness begins in the heart and mind (devotion to God) then is lived out in words and behavior (expressed in a life that is pleasing to Him). We adorn ourselves with godliness for God the Father and our Lord Jesus Christ because of our love for them and gratitude for what they have done for our salvation and everything we have been given for life now and in the future.

9. Let's see the details Paul gives about himself and why he was devoted to God in vv. 12-17.

   Why did Paul thank God (v. 12)?

   Paul was once what kind of man (v. 13)?

   Why was he shown mercy (v. 13)?

   What was poured out on Paul (v. 14)?

   What is a trustworthy statement that deserves dull acceptance (v. 15)?

   Paul was the worst what (v. 15)?

   For what reason was Paul shown mercy (v. 16)?

   Write Paul's response to God (v. 17) in the space below.

Focus on the Meaning: Amen—The word comes from a Hebrew root meaning, "to be firm, steady, trustworthy." It is used in the Old Testament by a congregation or an individual to accept both the validity of an oath and its consequences (see Numbers 5:22, Deuteronomy 27:15-16, Jeremiah 11:5) as well as a response to a benediction. By the time of the New Testament, the word was regularly used at the close of prayers and doxologies to agree with the ideas and sentiments that had just been expressed.

God showed Paul mercy (vv. 13, 16). Paul had not opposed Jesus Christ and His church because he wanted to dishonor God. Paul believed he was serving God by persecuting Christians. He was mistaken about who Jesus Christ was. "For this reason," God had mercy on him. Instead of getting punishment, God showed him mercy. Mercy is not getting what we deserve.

10. ***Deeper Discoveries (optional):*** Read Psalm 103:10-14 and Ephesians 2:3-7. What do these verses tell us about God's mercy towards us?

Focus on the Meaning: What is grace? Grace is that which God does for mankind through His Son, which mankind cannot earn, does not deserve, and will never merit. It is God's unmerited favor in spite of the response of humanity. It is summed up in the name, person, and work of the Lord Jesus Christ. (Chuck Swindoll)

11. What did Paul say about God's grace toward him (v. 14)? Why is that word picture encouraging to anyone who puts their faith in Jesus Christ?

12. Why does the "trustworthy saying" in v. 15 deserve "full acceptance?"

Focus on the Meaning: "Trustworthy saying" in Greek is *pistos ho logos*, literally, "faithful the word." The phrase is found only in the pastoral epistles. See also 1 Timothy 3:1; 2 Timothy 2:11; and Titus 3:8. It is used to describe statements that ought to be regarded as fully reliable—a nonnegotiable truth.

13. How was Paul an example of Christ's immense patience (v. 16)?

14. ***Deeper Discoveries (optional):*** Read about Paul's conversion in Acts 7:54–8:3; 9:1-31; 22:3-5; 22:19-20; 26:9-11; and Galatians 1:13-14. From the information given about Paul's life before he met Christ, why would Paul say that he was "the worst of sinners?"

> **Think About It:** Jesus Christ alone deserves the credit for the remarkable change in Paul's life, not Paul.

15. What can we know about our God from the "doxology" Paul wrote in v. 17?

What application will you make to adorn yourself with godliness?

> **Focus on the Meaning:** Godliness begins with God-centered devotion. It is a life given to God so that you desire God's will over your own will, or the way and spirit of the world. It means you consider pleasing God in all aspects of your ordinary, everyday life. You desire God to be at the center of your thoughts. It doesn't mean perfection. In Paul's words to the Corinthians in 1 Corinthians 10:31, "So whether you eat or drink or whatever you do, do it all for the glory of God." From this Godward attitude arises the character and conduct that we usually think of as godliness. So often we try to develop Christian character and conduct without taking the time to develop God-centered devotion. We try to please God without taking the time to walk with Him and develop a relationship with Him. This is impossible to do. (Jerry Bridges, adapted from *The Practice of Godliness*)

16. How have you experienced Christ's immense patience? Where would we be if God were not patient, merciful and gracious to us? Read 1 Timothy 2:3-4 and 2 Peter 3:9. Thank God for His immense patience with you this week. Pray for those in your sphere of influence who have still not trusted in Christ that they would respond to His amazing grace.

17. Devotion to God begins with love for Him and gratitude for what He has done. Those beautiful words in 1 Timothy 1:17 have been put to music. Go to YouTube.com and search for "Now unto the King Eternal." Listen to those songs to enhance your love for who God is. Tell God how much you love Him. Ask Him to fill your mind and heart with devotion to Him.

DAY THREE STUDY

Read 1 Timothy 1:1-20. Ask the Lord Jesus to teach you through His Word.

We will focus on vv. 3-7 and 18-20 in this session.

What does it mean?

18. Read 1 Timothy 1:3-6 and 4:1-2.

- What problems were plaguing the church in Ephesus? See also 2 Timothy 2:14-17. Note: "Certain people" includes both men and women. That comes into play later in the letter.

- What does this reveal about the nature and consequences of false teaching?

> **Focus on the Meaning:** We don't know exactly what the false teachers in Ephesus were teaching. ... [Whatever it was] simply generated questions ("speculations") for which there are no real answers, rather than contributing to the spiritual maturation of believers. ... The ultimate aim of a Bible teacher should not be to generate debate and controversy. It should be to cultivate the lives of his or her students, so that they manifest "love" in their daily living (v. 5). (*Dr. Constable's Notes on 1 Timothy 2020 Edition*, pp. 16-18)

19. ***Deeper Discoveries (optional):*** Read Paul's letter to the Ephesians, written 2-3 years before this one to Timothy. Notice the "truth and sound doctrine" this Ephesian church had already received about salvation, their membership as Jews and Gentiles in the Church, the power of God available to them for living a life that pleases Him, and the differences between godly and ungodly behavior.

20. False teaching in the church needs to be stopped. Sound doctrine must be emphasized. But, notice that Paul says the goal of doing so is love that comes from "a pure heart and a good conscience and a sincere faith" (v. 5). These words show up again in v. 19. What could it mean to have a...?

- "pure heart"—

- "good conscience"—

- "sincere faith"—

Focus on the Meaning: To have a good, or pure, conscience does not mean that we have never sinned or do not commit acts of sin. Rather, it means that the underlying direction and motive of life is to obey and please God, so that acts of sin are habitually recognized as such and faced before God. This is an aspect of devotion to God. Regarding the word "sincere," you can sincerely do a lot of bad things (drink poison, believe a lie, etc.) and reap the consequences. A sincere faith must be anchored to God's truth.

21. In 1 Timothy 1:4-5, Paul outlines 2 ways of determining whether a teaching is valid and true. Read the following summary:

    Focus on the Meaning: Paul paints a double contrast between speculation and faith in God's revelation and between controversy and love for one another. Here are two practical tests for us to apply to all teaching. The first is the test of faith: does it come from God, being in agreement with apostolic doctrine (so that it may be received by faith), or is it the product of fertile human imagination? The second is the test of love: does it promote unity in the body of Christ? ... Faith means that we receive it from God; love means that it builds up the church. The ultimate criteria by which to judge any teaching are whether it promotes the glory of God and the good of the church. (John Stott, *1 Timothy & Titus: Fighting the Good Fight,* p. 12)

    Does this summary help you understand verses 4-5 in discerning whether a certain teaching might be truth or error? Why or why not?

22. According to 1 Timothy 1:6-7, the false teachers, who may have been elders in the church that were once sound in their doctrine, had strayed and turned aside from the truth to "meaningless talk." Read vv. 6-7 in several translations.

    • What could Paul have meant by the phrase "meaningless talk?"

    • What would be the opposite of "meaningless talk?"

    Think About It: Wandering into the area of speculation in Bible Study can lead to purposeless rabbit trails and dangerous conclusions. According to Deuteronomy 29:29, the secret things belong to the Lord, but the things revealed belong to us. The secret things are things He has not revealed to us and doesn't need us to know. Instead, we should learn all that is revealed to us because they belong to us. There is so much we can know that is truth, while speculation about things God hasn't revealed is detrimental to our faith and can be destructive when we don't find the answer we want.

23. In 1 Timothy 1:18-20, what is the "good fight" Paul urged Timothy to fight? See also 1 Timothy 6:12.

24. Paul noted that some believers had shipwrecked their faith. Paul had handed Hymenaeus and Alexander over to Satan, removing them from the church fellowship. Hymenaeus' error is described in 2 Timothy 2:17-18. What is the error? Why would Paul do something like this? See also 2 Thessalonians 3:14-15.

Historical Insight: Resurrection has one meaning only, a bodily resurrection. Nobody ever used it to mean life after death or a ghost wandering around after death. It means the restoration of a dead body in a new immortal form. To the Greek mind, the body was evil; the soul was good. Death rescued the soul from the body. There was no place in this thinking for resurrection. (N.T. Wright, *The Resurrection of the Son of God*, p. 145)

What application will you make to adorn yourself with godliness?

25. Studying the Bible carefully using the inductive process (observation, interpretation, application) helps to avoid a focus on "meaningless talk" regarding spiritual truth. Ask the Lord to show you any false teaching that you have accepted because it sounded good. Ask Him to help you discover the truth about that teaching from the Bible. Trust Him to do that and watch what He does!

26. For the sake of the rest of the members, a local church body cannot support error-filled teaching. How do you determine whether you are hearing teaching that is true to the gospel or not? What are some of the "red flags" for which you can look or listen in someone's teaching?

Respond to the Lord about what you learned today.

DAY FOUR STUDY

Read 1 Timothy 1:1-20. Ask the Lord Jesus to teach you through His Word.

We will focus on vv. 7-11 in this session.

What does it mean?

The Law (1 Timothy 1:7-8) refers to the Mosaic Law found in the first five books of the Bible (aka the Torah), which was compiled by Moses. It can also refer to the whole Old Testament, which were the Scriptures of Paul's day. The Jews often referred to their Scriptures as "the Law and the Prophets" (Matthew 22:40).

27. According to 1 Timothy 1:8-11, the Mosaic Law had a purpose.

    • Read Galatians 3:19-24. What do you learn about the purpose and duration for the Law? See also Romans 7:7-8.

    • Could the Law produce righteousness in anyone abiding by it?

28. The Mosaic Law was given to reveal behavior that is not pleasing to God—ungodliness—so that the faithful believer will recognize that and choose to do what pleases God instead. What is declared ungodly behavior in 1 Timothy 1:9-10?

> **Scriptural Insight:** A former pastor of mine said that the law is like a mirror. It can show you that there is a problem, but it can't provide a solution. So, what role does the Mosaic Law play in a Christian's life? The Mosaic Law included 3 parts: the civil law governing how to run the nation of Israel, the moral law governing behavior, and the religious law governing a sinful human's relationship with a holy God. Christians are not under the civil law or the religious law. Christ fulfilled all the requirements of the religious law for us so we can now have a restored relationship with God based on our faith in Christ. But, we are still subject to God's moral law which existed way before the Mosaic Law was given to the Jews at Mt. Sinai. All the elements of God's moral law are included in the Mosaic Law and the New Testament teachings about what God considers to be right and wrong in His eyes (for example: Galatians 5; Ephesians 4-5; Colossians 3).

29. Besides what you learned in 1 Timothy 1:3-7, we also get a clue about what the false teachers were teaching the people in chapter 4. Read 1 Timothy 4:3-5. What do you learn?

Focus on the Meaning: One of the problems affecting the church in Ephesus was *legalism* or *asceticism* (1 Timothy 1:7 and 4:3-5). These are characterized by a denial of good things. The dictionary definition of asceticism is "practicing strict self-denial as a measure of personal and especially spiritual discipline." Legalism is "strict, often too strict and literal, adherence to law." As pastor Chuck Swindoll says, "Legalism invariably denies the principle of grace and exalts the pride of man." (Chuck Swindoll, *Growing Deep in the Christian Life,* p. 419)

The word *doctrine* (v. 10) is a key word in the pastoral epistles (1 Timothy, Titus, and 2 Timothy). Twenty-three of its fifty occurrences in the New Testament are found in Paul's writings, and of these twenty-three, seventeen are in the pastoral epistles. The word means "teaching."

30. Review what you learned in Lesson 1 Day Four Study. What does Paul mean by sound doctrine (v. 10)? See also 2 Timothy 1:8-10.

31. Why is it so important to maintain sound doctrine and refute false teachings? Look for your answer within 1 Timothy 1:3-20.

32. Consider the connection between sound doctrine and godliness / godly living.

   • Why would sound doctrine likely lead to godliness?

   • Why would departing from sound doctrine likely lead to ungodliness?

What application will you make to adorn yourself with godliness?

33. The popular British author C. S. Lewis said that moral collapse follows upon spiritual collapse.

   • What steps do you take to make sure your thinking and behavior is based on sound doctrine?

- In what ways does the teaching you have received encourage you towards godly living?

- What part does the will play in choosing to practice what you have learned?

34. In Lesson Two, we saw several evidences of godliness displayed—devotion to God expressed in a life pleasing to Him. Feel free to add to the list in the chart below. Choose one example of godliness from this passage. Ask the Lord Jesus to give you a desire for that in your life and to adorn you with that. He has the power to make it happen.

Verse(s)	What godliness looks like
v. 4	Devoted to advancing God's work
v. 5	Having a pure heart, a good conscience, and a sincere faith that encourages love for others
v. 16-17	Giving Christ the glory for what He does in your life
vv. 18-19	Fight the battle against error well, holding on to faith and a good conscience

Respond to the Lord about what you learned today.

Recommended: Listen to the podcast "Godliness Flows from Knowing Christ" after doing this lesson to reinforce what you have learned. Use the following listener guide.

Godliness Flows from Knowing Christ

CHRISTIANITY IS CHRIST!

- It's not a lifestyle. It's not rules of conduct. It's not a society of people who are joined together by the sprinkling or covering of water. Christianity is a relationship with the Lord Jesus Christ.

- The title "the Christ" is from the Greek word *christos,* a translation of the Hebrew term "Messiah" meaning "anointed one." Christians are followers of Jesus, who is the Christ.

- If you have heard the good news of the gospel and believed that Jesus is the Son of God who gave Himself for your sins, you have eternal life just by believing in Him as Savior. But more than salvation, Jesus Christ calls us into a close relationship with Himself.

- Jesus Christ is our *master*—the one to whom we should willingly give our obedience. He is our *model* of how to live as humans in a dependent relationship with God, and He is our *mentor* in walking with us to show us how to adorn ourselves with godliness.

- Jesus' disciples 2000 years ago were no different than we are except they physically beheld the risen Christ. We must see Him through eyes of faith and allow the Gospels to leap off the page revealing our Lord because Christianity is Christ!

UNDERSTANDING THE GOSPEL MESSAGE AS AN ACCOMPLISHED FACT

- We humans have a spiritual problem that can be compared to death caused by a fatal disease. It's a two-fold problem. Sin is the disease. Everyone has it. And, death is the result of the disease. We are born spiritually dead sinners. Our double whammy problem demanded a two-fold solution. The great news is that God acted on our behalf.

  ✓ For the problem of sin, people need sin to be removed and replaced with righteousness. *God's answer is Christ's death on the cross.* Because of His finished work on the cross, we can now be cured of the disease.

  ✓ For the problem of death, people need the restoration of life. *God's answer is Christ's resurrection.* We can now be given life that is forever.

- The Gospel message included the answer to both spiritual problems.

  "Jesus Christ **laid down** his life **for** you...so that he could **give** his life **to** you...so that he could **live** his life **through** you." (Ian Thomas, *The Saving Life of Christ*)

WHAT FAITH IS AND IS NOT

- Faith is not a blind belief or mindless gullibility. It is not a life of passivity and doing nothing. Faith is also not a religious feeling like a tingle or a high from performing some ritual.

- Faith is a "belief, trust, and commitment of mind and heart to something or someone."
  - ✓ Faith is **intelligent**. That means first you need to know about the something or someone. It is based on information about the object of your faith.
  - ✓ Faith is also **decisive**. It involves the element of assent or agreement that the information about that someone or something is true.
  - ✓ Faith **requires an act of the will**. Any conscious choice that involves trust or dependence on someone or something requires a deliberate action to both trust the information and act on it.
- Simply put, faith is a full commitment to Christ. We are to respond to His action by saying yes to faith in Jesus Christ and jumping into the new life God has for us.

- God offers you salvation from the destruction caused by sin. He offers you this salvation by His grace that is given to you. Grace is an undeserved gift. By God's grace, you are saved through your faith alone. It is the gift of God—not by works, so that no one can boast of their efforts. *Ephesians 2:8-9*

- Through getting to know Him and what He has done for us, we discover that the treasure we have in Jesus Christ is worth devoting our lives to Him.

DEVOTION TO GOD GROWS AS WE LEARN HOW MUCH WE CAN TRUST HIM.

- There are two aspects to trusting God.
  - ✓ 1) **Trusting God while you do your part His way.** To do your part His way involves your knowing what His way is. That comes from knowing what He says. That comes from reading and studying the Bible. You trust that His way is the best way so you are willing to step forward and do your part His way. Sometimes that involves just waiting.
  - ✓ 2) **Trusting Him to do His part alongside what you are doing.** That's trusting God to work in the background of life and make things happen in those areas over which you have no direct access. You trust Him to work and are patient to let Him do so.
- Knowing God and trusting Him increases your devotion to Him, your loyal love for Him. And, that leads to expressing your devotion in a life that pleases Him—a life of godliness. Godliness flows from knowing Christ.

  "Now to the King eternal, immortal, invisible, the only God, be honor and glory for ever and ever! Amen." (1 Timothy 1:17)

The treasure you have in Jesus Christ is more powerful and valuable than anything you could substitute for Him. After chasing everything the world has to offer, nothing is more satisfying than Him. You can say to Him, "My treasure in you, Lord Jesus, is more powerful and valuable than anything I could substitute for You. Please confirm that in my heart." Then, watch what He does!

Let Jesus satisfy your heart with such love for God that you will want to live a life that pleases Him.

3: Dressed for Worshiping God in Community

1 Timothy 2:1-15

DAY ONE STUDY—GET THE BIG PICTURE

Ask the Lord Jesus to teach you through His Word.

What does the Bible say?

Read the Bible passage below (NIV) including verses from the last lesson. Use your own method (colored pencils, lines, shapes) to mark 1) anything that grabs your attention, 2) words you want to understand, and 3) topics you have seen before in this letter. Draw arrows between thoughts that connect. Put a star ✱ next to anything you think relates to godliness.

1 *15 Here is a trustworthy saying that deserves full acceptance: Christ Jesus came into the world to save sinners—of whom I am the worst. 16 But for that very reason I was shown mercy so that in me, the worst of sinners, Christ Jesus might display his immense patience as an example for those who would believe in him and receive eternal life. 17 Now to the King eternal, immortal, invisible, the only God, be honor and glory for ever and ever. Amen.*

18 Timothy, my son, I am giving you this command in keeping with the prophecies once made about you, so that by recalling them you may fight the battle well, 19 holding on to faith and a good conscience, which some have rejected and so have suffered shipwreck with regard to the faith. 20 Among them are Hymenaeus and Alexander, whom I have handed over to Satan to be taught not to blaspheme.

2 *1 I urge, then, first of all, that petitions, prayers, intercession and thanksgiving be made for all people— 2 for kings and all those in authority, that we may live peaceful and quiet lives in all godliness and holiness. 3 This is good, and pleases God our Savior, 4 who wants all people to be saved and to come to a knowledge of the truth. 5 For there is one God and one mediator between God and mankind, the man Christ Jesus, 6 who gave himself as a ransom for all people. This has now been witnessed to at the proper time. 7 And for this purpose I was appointed a herald and an apostle—I am telling the truth, I am not lying—and a true and faithful teacher of the Gentiles.*

8 Therefore I want the men everywhere to pray, lifting up holy hands without anger or disputing. 9 I also want the women to dress modestly, with decency and propriety, adorning themselves, not with elaborate hairstyles or gold or pearls or expensive clothes, 10 but with good deeds, appropriate for women who profess to worship God.

11 A woman should learn in quietness and full submission. 12 I do not permit a woman to teach or to assume authority over a man; she must be quiet. 13 For Adam was formed first, then Eve. 14 And Adam was not the one deceived; it was the woman who was deceived and became a sinner. 15 But women will be saved through childbearing—if they continue in faith, love and holiness with propriety.

1. What grabbed your attention from 1 Timothy 2:1-15?

2. What verses or specific words do you want to understand better?

3. What words or phrases are repeated in this passage? Give verses.

4. What topics (if any) in this passage have we studied in previous lessons? Give verses.

5. What verses illustrate or help you understand what godliness looks like?

6. ***Adorn yourself with godliness:*** From this lesson's passage (1 Timothy 2:1-15), choose one verse to dwell upon all week long. Write it in the space below. Ask God to teach you through this verse.

Respond to the Lord about what you learned today.

DAY TWO STUDY

Read 1 Timothy 2:1-15. Ask the Lord Jesus to teach you through His Word.

We will focus on vv. 1-7 in this session.

What does it mean?

As a representative of the apostle Paul, Timothy was *under* Paul, but *over* the elders of the church, in his authority. Therefore, he had the authority to order worship and appoint elders and deacons.

In v. 1, Paul used four words for prayer: petitions, prayers, intercession, and thanksgiving. The words are not significantly different. The grouping of these four words together is to emphasize the need for all kinds of prayer—whether for oneself, another person (intercession), the community, or simply thanking God for all that He has done for you.

> **Scriptural Insight:** Prayer is so very important, because it invites God into the situation we are praying about, and it secures His working on behalf of those in need. Christians must not fail to take advantage of this supernatural resource at their disposal—by neglecting prayer. This verse (v. 1) should answer the question of whether we should pray for the unsaved. "All men" certainly includes them. (*Dr. Constable's Notes on 1 Timothy 2020 Edition,* p. 38)

7. Paul urged that prayers be offered for kings and all those in authority, especially governmental authorities.

   - According to 1 Timothy 2:2-3, why are we to pray for our leaders?

   - According to Romans 13:1-7, why are we to pray for our leaders? See also Proverbs 21:1.

> **Historical Insight:** These instructions are remarkable. Few authorities at the time were Christians. And, the reigning Roman emperor Nero was cruel to Christians in Rome. Persecution of the church throughout the empire was ramping up so Christians were likely becoming apprehensive.

8. One of the purposes of praying for our governmental leaders is that we may live "peaceful and quiet lives" (v. 2).

> **From the Greek:** "Peaceful" means what you would expect—tranquil. "Quiet" (Gr., *hesychios*) means "tranquility arising from within." It does not mean whisper, silent, or bland. "Quiet" carries the idea of causing no disturbance to others (see vv. 11-12).

   - How does being able to live peaceful and quiet lives help us to carry out our purpose in the world as Christians?

- Why does this please God (vv. 3-4)?

> **Think About It:** Though cultures may promote other priorities, for the Christian what is good and acceptable in God's sight should take precedence in all things. There is nothing in this text, or in any other, that would limit the truly universal interpretation of God wanting "all men" to be saved. (*Dr. Constable's Notes on 1 Timothy 2020 Edition*, p. 39)

9. Looking at vv. 5-6,

- What truth does God want all men to know? This firmly declared truth is one of the most significant verses of the New Testament.

- Define the words "mediator" and "ransom."

- Why do we need a mediator?

- How did Jesus serve as our mediator? See also Romans 5:8-11.

- What ransom price did Jesus pay for our release?

> **Focus on the Meaning:** This is something that people have found hard to accept throughout history. In Paul's day, the Jews looked to Moses or angels as mediators, and the Gnostics [Greeks who sought a higher spiritual experience through secret knowledge] looked to intermediary deities (aeons). In our own day, [certain denominations] look to dead "saints" for mediatorial benefits, and Buddhists look to their ancestors. Nevertheless, the teaching of verse 5 is clear: the only "mediator" between the God and people is Jesus Christ (John 14:6). (*Dr. Constable's Notes on 1 Timothy 2020 Edition*, p. 41)

10. Because God wants all people to be saved (Jews and non-Jews), what commission was Paul given by God? See also Acts 9:15-16; 22:14-15; and 26:15-18.

Think About It: Paul's ministry to Gentiles helped to fulfill God's covenant to Abraham to bless all the families of the earth (Genesis 12:1-3; Galatians 3:14). If you are a Gentile Christian, thank God for His invitation to you to share in the covenant.

What application will you make to adorn yourself with godliness?

11. Who would be the equivalent of "kings and those in authority" today (1 Timothy 2:2)? Spend some time this week praying for those on your list—for their salvation if unbelievers, for their obedience to God if believers, and for them to carry out the godly purposes of their positions based on what you learned in the questions above.

12. Have you been taught that you must go through someone more spiritual than you in order to reach God? Dwell on 1 Timothy 2:5-6. Read also Ephesians 2:6; and Hebrews 4:15-16. How does it impact you to know that Jesus is your mediator? That He gave His life as a ransom for you? Feel free to use any creative means to describe how you feel about this fact.

Respond to the Lord about what you learned today.

DAY THREE STUDY

Read 1 Timothy 2:1-15. Ask the Lord Jesus to teach you through His Word.

We will focus on vv. 8-10 in this session.

What does it mean?

> **Focus on the Meaning:** In the NIV translation, anything addressed just to men is translated "men" or "brothers." Anything addressed just to women is translated "women" or "wives" depending on the context. That which applies to everyone is usually translated "all people" or "brothers and sisters." Not all translations make this distinction.

The setting for this chapter is the gathering together of the people of God in their local church communities to worship God and continue learning truth from the church leaders. Keep this in mind as you study the passage.

13. Continuing the emphasis on praying together that Paul started in v. 1:

- How are the men everywhere (in all the churches) to pray?

- The words "holy" and "holiness" (v. 15) mean "to be set apart from sin and to God." "Hands" represent what we do—our attitude and behavior. What could it mean to pray with "holy hands?"

> **Scriptural Insight:** In New Testament culture, a common prayer posture was to stand with hands lifted up (Luke 24:50). Other prayer postures mentioned in the Bible are bowing, kneeling, and lying prostrate (face down). Paul was not commanding the men to pray with physically upraised hands. He simply was describing public praying as the Christians commonly practiced it in his day. ... "Holy," "anger," and "disputing" all point to a metaphorical use of "hands." (*Dr. Constable's Notes on 1 Timothy 2020 Edition,* p. 45)

14. In 1 Timothy 2:8, we read that men are to pray without anger or disputing, which would be disruptive to worshiping together. The Greek word translated "disputing" means "a deliberating or questioning of (possibly arguing about) what is true; skeptical questions or criticisms." What did you learn from 1 Timothy chapter 1 that could give clues about this being a problem for the men in the church?

15. ***Deeper Discoveries (optional):*** Read Matthew 5:23-24; Matthew 6:12; and 1 Peter 3:7. How can our relationship with others impact our prayer and worship?

The beginning of v. 9 in the Greek is "in like manner." That means Paul is continuing to address disruptive behavior in the church community as he did in v. 8. The next thing he addressed is how women are to adorn themselves for the church worship gathering.

Paul used 3 specific words in the first half of v. 9 to describe how women ARE to dress: modest, decency, and propriety. Literally, the text says "In like manner also women to adorn themselves in modest apparel with reverence for others (decency) and soundness of mind (propriety)." Let's look at those three words.

16. *Modest*:

- Define modest.

- What could it mean today to dress in "modest apparel?"

17. *Decency:* The word translated decency (Gr. *aidos*) can mean "reverence, regard for others, respect." Reverence for others, regard for others, and respect means you have the other person in mind more than pleasing yourself. How could a woman choosing to dress with modesty enhance the corporate worship experience of Christ for everyone, especially for the men also participating in the worship of Christ?

18. *Propriety:* The word translated propriety means "sound thinking and self-control." It carries the idea of taking careful thought and not being flippant or reckless. That fits with the rest of verse 9. Having respect and regard for others involves more than just modesty in a sexual sense. Read verse 9 again.

- What should NOT be the focus of a woman's adornment?

- What do "elaborate hairstyles, gold, pearls, and expensive clothes" represent?

- How could that be disruptive to a community worshiping God? See also James 2:2-6.

Focus on the Meaning: There isn't anything inherently wrong with braided hair, wearing jewelry, or dressing nicely. Yet, elaborate hairstyles, jewelry, and clothing usually represents wealth and a higher social status. That's not as true today as it was in the first century AD. We humans like to make rules for everyone, so you can read in church history that women were encouraged to wear drab colors, no makeup, no jewelry, and certainly have no skin showing. That is the wrong response. God designed lots of His creatures with beautiful colors. He created women with beautiful features and an attractive shape. He likes color. The issue is whether you are pointing people to Christ more than to yourself. It's a heart issue.

19. If your adornment is not to represent your rank and wealth,

- In what other ways ARE women to adorn themselves (v. 10 and the end of v. 15)?

- Why? In other words, whom / what should your adornment represent? Remember our definition of godliness.

20. **Deeper Discoveries (optional):** Read 1 Peter 3:2-4. How does this passage compare with 1 Timothy 2:9-10?

What application will you make to adorn yourself with godliness?

21. Considering what can be disruptive in a worship service:

- Have the displays of wealth, fashion, and cultural status by women in your church service ever caused a problem for you in worship? What kinds of things distract you in a worship service? Ask the Lord to show you how to keep your focus on devotion to Him and love for your fellow worshipers.

- Are you one of those who might be distracting to others around you? Do you adorn yourself with symbols of power that reveal your wealth, cultural status, or self-promotion? Your adornment reveals who you are and Whose you are. Ask the Lord to show you where your focus on looks might be overshadowing your love for others.

22. *Considering women adorned with good works:* Think of women you know who are "adorned with good works" even more than just their looks. Why do you describe them that way? How would leading this kind of life be attractive to any nonbeliever so that the gospel may be spread?

Respond to the Lord about what you learned today.

DAY FOUR STUDY

Read 1 Timothy 2:1-15. Ask the Lord Jesus to teach you through His Word.

We will focus on vv. 11-15 in this session.

What does it mean?

> **From the Greek:** Within the context, we have some translation issues not apparent in a quick read of the English version. ... the word *gyne* in Koine Greek, translated "woman" here, means either women or wives. The Greek did not have separate words to distinguish the two. Only context tells which. If there is a husband in the context, "wife" is preferred. It is unclear in this passage if Paul is addressing wives as he does in 1 Corinthians 14:34-35 or [if he is addressing] all women. Roman civil law at the time did require wifely deference to husbands in public. Wives were not permitted to publicly question their husbands. Such behavior would be disruptive to the worship service. (Dr. Sandra Glahn, *"1 Corinthians 14: Are Women Really Supposed to Be Silent in Church?"* accessed at Bible.org)

23. According to verse 11,

- What is the one thing every Christian woman is encouraged to do?

- What is to be her attitude when taught?

24. Regarding "in quietness" (v. 11), read the "Scriptural Insight" then answer the question that follows.

> **Scriptural Insight:** What does "in quietness" mean? The same Greek word *hesuchia* translated "peace" in v. 2, is also used in vv. 11-12. How this word is used elsewhere in the New Testament adds insight to how it is used here. In Acts 22:2, *hesuchia* carries the idea of having a tranquility from within so as to be willing to listen. The opposite would be a restless spirit that is quick to argue. In 2 Thessalonians 3:12, it is translated as "settle down" with the idea of not causing a disturbance to others. The opposite would be "always engaged in controversy and provoking negative responses." Paul's use of *hesuchia* fits with the rest of chapter 2 regarding what is disruptive to the worship community and chapter 1 regarding false teaching.

How does having this kind of attitude toward learning truth benefit a woman?

25. Regarding "full submission" (v. 11),

- Look up the definition of "submission" and write it below.

- What is involved in biblical submission to authority? See also 1 Peter 2:21-23; 3:1-6.

- Is the Bible's view of submission like the world's view of submission? Why or why not?

Think About It: Basically, in quietness and full submission means that you are teachable. And, God gives biblical authority to leaders for the purpose of building up others.

26. What was not permitted (v. 12)? Note: Remember that this is in the context of the public worship gathering. This is not referring to businesses, seminaries, or any other arena where men and women work together outside of the local church. There are no biblical restrictions on the roles of the sexes in social and civic life.

Scriptural Insight: The verbs "teach" and "exercise authority" are in the present tense in the Greek text, which implies a continuing ministry rather than a single instance of ministry. ... "Teach" has in view the teaching of the Scriptures. The Greek word translated "assume authority" means to act on one's own authority or to act in an autocratic manner. To exercise authority, in this unbiblical way, would be to submit to no higher (male) authority in the church, or to not be answerable or accountable to the church's male leadership. Paul was forbidding women, in this passage, from regularly teaching men in local church corporate worship. Paul approved of women teaching women and children (Titus 2:3-5; 2 Timothy 1:5), and instructing men privately (Acts 18:26). (*Dr. Constable's Notes on 1 Timothy 2020 Edition,* pp. 50-52)

27. We cannot fully understand what Paul meant by this statement because we don't have all the background that he had already taught and practiced in the churches.

- Going back to "full submission" (v. 11) though, who is our example of submission to the will of God? How is He our example?

- What would be the benefit of considering the Lord's example when it comes to understanding what v. 12 means in the local church gathering?

Think About It: God designed men in the beginning (Genesis 2) to learn from Him and lead others on His behalf. To love someone means doing what is best for the one loved. That's what God does for us. We as women should love our Christian brothers and want what is best for them more than what we want. If it is God's will that men should teach men in the local church, why would we fight Him on that?

28. **Deeper Discoveries (optional):** Whereas pagan women were rarely educated, all Christian women, both Jew and Gentile, were carefully and freely instructed in the Scriptures and became significant in the spread of the gospel and establishment of local churches. Read Acts 16:14-15, 40; Acts 18:18, 26; Romans 16:1-2; and 1 Corinthians 16:19. What roles did women have in the early church? Can you see yourself taking on one of these roles?

Scriptural Insight: In Old Testament times, women served in the doorway of the Tabernacle (Exodus 38:8). They served as prophetesses (Miriam, Deborah, Huldah) and led other women in praise and worship. Their songs of praise are recorded in Scripture (Miriam, Deborah, Hannah, Mary). Many women sang in the temple choirs (Nehemiah 7:66-67). Psalm 68:11 says that women proclaimed the Lord's word as "a mighty throng." I like that!

29. Focusing on 1 Timothy 2:12-14. God established a human authority structure at creation that has not changed, although marred by sin. God could have created Adam and Eve at the same instant, but He did not—by His own choice and purpose. As I once heard, "It's how God decided to organize His team." Read Genesis 2:18-25 and 1 Corinthians 11:3, 8-9. What authority structure has God established?

Scriptural Insight: The priority of the male in creation reflects God's appointed *order* for His creation, not male superiority. Man has the responsibility of headship (1 Corinthians 11:3; Ephesians 5:21), and woman has the responsibility of being a "fitting helper" (Genesis 2:18). Each supplies what is lacking in the other. They are complementary because they are distinct. (*Dr. Constable's Notes on 1 Timothy 2020 Edition,* p. 138)

In 1 Timothy 2:14, Paul referenced Eve being deceived. Other references to the order of creation in 1 Corinthians 11:3, 8-9 and Ephesians 5:23 do not mention deception at all. But, some wrongly teach that women are more easily deceived than men because of what happened in Genesis 3.

Scriptural Insight: The man and woman in [Genesis 3] ... both rebelled. ... Being seduced by evil is a human thing, not a woman thing—as Paul mentions when warning the Corinthians (2 Corinthians 11:3). The Bible does not teach that because Eve was deceived, all women are more easily deceived than men. Nor does the Scripture teach that all women excel at seducing and deceiving (these ideas are contradictions, anyway—one cannot be a master of deception while also being easily duped)." (Sandra Glahn, *"Biblical Womanhood": What is a Woman?* accessed online at Bible.org)

Deception instigated by both men and women was a problem in all of the New Testament churches and is still a problem today. The answer to deception is standing firm on the truth of the gospel.

WHAT ABOUT 1 TIMOTHY 2:15?

In Lesson 1, I told you that some verses in this letter are difficult to understand and may remain a mystery until we get to heaven. Paul's words in 1 Timothy 2:15 (the first part) fit that category. No one really knows exactly what Paul was trying to communicate there. Scholars consider verse 15 to be one of the most difficult New Testament verses to interpret.

What it cannot mean

We know v. 15 is not a promise that Christian women will be kept physically safe through the process of childbirth. Many Christian women have died in childbirth. Since God doesn't lie, He certainly wouldn't make an empty promise to women believers. And, all are saved by grace through faith in Jesus Christ, not through any works. So, we know it is not a promise that women will be saved through the bearing of children, especially since many Christian women have never born children.

Some take the childbearing to refer to Eve's childbearing, as the mother of all the living, and eventually Jesus Christ. Since both men and women are saved through Christ, this doesn't seem to fit the context.

What it could mean

The Greek word translated "saved" can also be translated "healed," "preserved," or "deliverance from danger." The danger doesn't always mean physical danger but could be spiritual danger, something mentioned in both letters. False teaching, traditional tales (1 Timothy 1:3-4), opposition to submission (1 Timothy 2:11; 6:3-5), and weak women who are laden with guilt (2 Timothy 3:6-7) are among those spiritual dangers.

Since the verses before this one refer to deception, that seems to be the best fit. Some deception related to childbearing was affecting the women of Ephesus. Childbirth in the ancient world carried legitimate fears of writhing and death. The Ephesian women had traditionally depended upon their goddess Artemis to deliver them safely through childbirth. It would be no surprise that their old life still clung to them when it came to this sometimes-terrifying experience. The following information about the culture of Ephesus gives insight into what Paul possibly meant by his declaration.

> **Historical Insight:** Artemis has her name from the fact that she makes people 'Artemeas' meaning sound, well, or delivered…Pestilential diseases and sudden deaths are imputed to these gods. It may seem strange for one persona to be linked with both delivery and death. Yet this makes more sense when we consider the sorts of prayers women offered: "Deliver me safely or kill me quickly!" Another word that shows up when Artemis is mentioned is 'save.' The ideas of 'deliver' and 'save' do go hand in hand. And in [one ancient] writing, we see with relative frequency references to Artemis Ephesia as 'savior.' In addition to his writings, we find references to 'Artemis Savior'—twenty of them! —in ancient inscription evidence. So, Artemis Ephesia is one who saves or delivers. And she is deemed to have the power to deliver a first-century woman through the most dangerous of passages—childbirth. (Sandra Glahn, *"Who Was Artemis and Why Does It Matter? Part II,"* accessed from Bible.org)

So, maybe Paul is encouraging the Ephesian Christian women to call upon the Lord God for the greatest fear they had—to be "delivered through childbirth"—and NOT to call upon Artemis Ephesia as they had done in the past. Such dependence on Artemis would be based upon deception and not truth, a reason for Paul to mention deception in v. 14.

Since only God really knows exactly what Paul was trying to communicate, we'll leave this with the possible explanations above.

30. We don't know what the first half of verse 15 means, but we can certainly understand the second half, which is still addressed to women. The word translated "continue" means to remain and not depart from.

   - In what are we to remain in and not depart from?

   - How does that related to verses 9-12?

What application will you make to adorn yourself with godliness?

31. The first half of 1 Timothy 2:11 says women have the freedom in Christ to receive instruction and learn the truths essential to the Christian faith and how to live them out in godliness. To learn with a tranquil heart and in submission to truth means you are teachable. God loves it when we are teachable.

   - Read Acts 17:11 and 1 Thessalonians 2:13. What do you learn about being teachable?

   - Do you consider yourself a teachable person? Why or why not?

   - Would others consider you a teachable person? If you don't know, ask someone close to you this question.

   - Since you are encouraged to learn everything you can about Christ through His Word, ask the Lord to help you take advantage of this wonderful privilege with a teachable attitude. He will answer "Yes!" to that prayer.

32. Do you struggle with submission to learning from male church leaders? Talk to the Lord about this. Why are you hesitant? Where is your devotion and trust? Ask Him to help you have godly thinking about this that will please Him.

33. In Lesson Three, we saw several evidences of godliness displayed—devotion to God expressed in a life pleasing to Him. Feel free to add to the list in the chart below. Choose one example of godliness from this passage. Ask the Lord Jesus to give you a desire for that in your life and to adorn you with that. He has the power to make it happen.

Verse(s)	What godliness looks like
vv. 1-2	*Praying for kings and all those in authority to obey God*
V 2	*Living a peaceful and quiet life in all godliness and holiness*
v. 8	*Worshiping God in holiness without unresolved anger or questioning what is true*
v. 9	*Dressing modestly, with regard for others more than for yourself*
vv. 9-10	*Doing good deeds that reflect your devotion to God*
v. 11	*Learn in an attitude of tranquility and willingness to learn, be teachable*
v. 12	*Respect the proper spiritual authority of a man over a man in the worship service.*
v. 15	*Stand strong in faith, love, and holiness with propriety*

Respond to the Lord about what you learned today.

Recommended: Listen to the podcast "Loyalty to God Affects How You Adorn Yourself" after doing this lesson to reinforce what you have learned. Use the following listener guide.

Loyalty to God Affects How You Adorn Yourself

JESUS DEMONSTRATED GOD'S LOVE FOR WOMEN.

- The Lord Jesus demonstrated in His life on earth how much He loved and valued women. He taught them truth about God, forgave them for their sins, accepted them in His circle of followers, and gave new life to them after His resurrection. Women who knew Him loved Him and wanted to follow and serve Him!

THE APOSTLES CONTINUED JESUS' ATTITUDE TOWARD WOMEN.

- Every local church incorporated women into the body of believers and taught them the truths of the faith along with the men. Women played a significant role in the church's expansion. They supported the church through hospitality and financial gifts. Women were active in speaking God's word (prophesying) and praying in the public worship service alongside the male members of the congregation.

- Only two restrictions were placed on women in the church. Women are restricted from the ongoing, authoritative teaching of a woman over a man in the church and holding the position of elder. Both of these are consistent with God's activity in the Old Testament. *1 Timothy 2:11; 3:1-7*

FREEDOM WITHIN BOUNDARIES

- Eve, the first woman, was deceived by Satan about why God had placed a restriction on that tree. Eve wanted what wasn't God's will for her or for Adam, either. *1 Timothy 2:12-14*

- Christian women have the freedom to learn every aspect of the Bible from Genesis to Revelation and can minister in many ways to many people, using our spiritual gifts to teach in the Body of Christ under the authority of the elders.

- Demanding freedom outside of the boundaries God has set always leads to straying from devotion to the Lord, from loyalty to Him. Your loyalty to God affects whether you will adorn yourself with godliness or with ungodliness.

TRUTH #1: JESUS DESERVES YOUR LOYALTY.

- The moment you trust in Jesus Christ as your savior, you get a new life fused together with His and a new identity. You are now said to be in Christ, a Child of God, one of God's saints, totally accepted and loved by Him.

- You are set free to live a radically different kind of life. And, in that freedom, you have a choice, "Who are you going to serve with your life now?" God or yourself?

TRUTH #2: LOYALTY REQUIRES HUMILITY.

- In the New Testament, humility refers to how you think of yourself. It pictures a servant bowing before her master.

- Humility is associated with gentleness. Gentleness carries the idea of strength under control. It is the outworking of humility and a work of the Holy Spirit. *Matthew 11:28-29; Ephesians 4:1-2*

- You choose humility before God by recognizing His authority over you. You are willing to trust God and accept His dealings with you as good without fighting Him on it.

- Humility is the opposite of self-assertiveness and self-interest. It is recognizing that God has given you the genetics, intelligence, and opportunity to do some things well.

TRUTH #3: HUMILITY LEADS TO OBEDIENCE.

- What good is a servant who refuses to obey? Or, who is out there trumpeting herself and her own will, and occasionally remembering to do what Jesus wants?

- When Paul wrote in 1 Timothy 2:11 that women should learn in quietness and full submission, he was referring to humility and obedience. God gave us women our gift of verbal communication. He expects our use of words to honor Him and teach about Him. But, sometimes, He wants us to be quiet and learn from others. The purpose for God's command is to benefit others. It is not to demean women.

- What are some hindrances to our obedience? One is lack of understanding of God's commands. Another hindrance is selectively choosing what we will obey. That leads us to being what the Bible describes as weak-willed women, always learning but never able to recognize truth for what it really is. Not seeing the ugliness of our sin also hinders obedience.

- Humility is the decision you make in your mind that you are not God, that Jesus is your master, and you serve Him by obedience to Him. That leads to a life that pleases Him.

TRUTH #4: OBEDIENCE OFFERS PROTECTION.

- Obedience is necessary to protect yourself from those who distort the truth and draw you away from Jesus and His way of approaching life. *Acts 20:28-31*

- When you have humbled yourself before Jesus as your master and have chosen to obey His commands revealed to you in the Bible, you will be able to recognize truth from anything that is distorted. But, when you resist the discipline that comes from obedience, you're vulnerable to embracing whatever new teaching that comes along as a fad or a cultural adaptation, and you cannot recognize the truth when you see it.

Loyalty affects how you adorn yourself with godliness or with all those other options out there that offer nothing lasting. Jesus as Lord deserves our loyalty. Loyalty requires humility. Humility leads to obedience. And, obedience offers protection from being sucked into every wave of teaching that exalts the individual over God.

Let Jesus satisfy your heart with such love for God that you will want to live a life that pleases Him.

4: The Fabric for Servant-Leadership

1 Timothy 3:1-16

DAY ONE STUDY—GET THE BIG PICTURE

Ask the Lord Jesus to teach you through His Word.

What does the Bible say?

Read the Bible passage below (NIV). Use your own method (colored pencils, lines, shapes) to mark 1) anything that grabs your attention, 2) words you want to understand, and 3) topics you have seen before in this letter. Draw arrows between thoughts that connect. Put a star ✱ next to anything you think relates to godliness.

3 *[1] Here is a trustworthy saying: Whoever aspires to be an overseer desires a noble task. [2] Now the overseer is to be above reproach, faithful to his wife, temperate, self-controlled, respectable, hospitable, able to teach, [3] not given to drunkenness, not violent but gentle, not quarrelsome, not a lover of money. [4] He must manage his own family well and see that his children obey him, and he must do so in a manner worthy of full respect. [5] (If anyone does not know how to manage his own family, how can he take care of God's church?) [6] He must not be a recent convert, or he may become conceited and fall under the same judgment as the devil. [7] He must also have a good reputation with outsiders, so that he will not fall into disgrace and into the devil's trap.*

[8] In the same way, deacons are to be worthy of respect, sincere, not indulging in much wine, and not pursuing dishonest gain. [9] They must keep hold of the deep truths of the faith with a clear conscience. [10] They must first be tested; and then if there is nothing against them, let them serve as deacons.

[11] In the same way, the women are to be worthy of respect, not malicious talkers but temperate and trustworthy in everything.

[12] A deacon must be faithful to his wife and must manage his children and his household well. [13] Those who have served well gain an excellent standing and great assurance in their faith in Christ Jesus.

[14] Although I hope to come to you soon, I am writing you these instructions so that, [15] if I am delayed, you will know how people ought to conduct themselves in God's household, which is the church of the living God, the pillar and foundation of the truth. [16] Beyond all question, the mystery from which true godliness springs is great:

He appeared in the flesh, was vindicated by the Spirit, was seen by angels, was preached among the nations, was believed on in the world, was taken up in glory.

1. What grabbed your attention from 1 Timothy 3:1-16?

2. What verses or specific words do you want to understand better?

3. What words or phrases are repeated in this passage? Give verses.

4. What topics (if any) in this passage have we studied in previous lessons? Give verses.

5. What verses illustrate or help you understand what godliness looks like?

6. ***Adorn yourself with godliness:*** From this lesson's passage (1 Timothy 3:1-16), choose one verse to dwell upon all week long. Write it in the space below. Ask God to teach you through this verse.

Respond to the Lord about what you learned today.

Day Two Study

Read 1 Timothy 3:1-16. Ask the Lord Jesus to teach you through His Word.

Today, we will focus on vv. 1-7.

What does it mean?

> **From the Greek:** The term overseer (*episkopos*), often translated "bishop," is only one of several words used in the New Testament to describe church leaders. "Elders" (*presbyteroi*) is by far the most common. Other terms such as "rulers" (*proistamenoi*, Romans 12:8; 1 Thessalonians 5:12), "leaders" (*hegoumenois*, Hebrews 13:17) and "pastors" (*poimenas*, Ephesians 4:11; Acts. 20:28; 1 Peter 5:2) are also used. Though each of these terms may describe a different facet of leadership, they all seem to be used interchangeably in the New Testament to designate the same office. This office is different from that of deacons. *(The Bible Knowledge Commentary New Testament*, p. 736)

Though various translations give a different title to this office (elder, overseer, bishop), we will use the term *elder* in this lesson because that is the most common use. The history of the elder office in the church goes back to the elder office in ancient Israel. The Jews had continued this organization in their synagogues, which they began during the Babylonian Captivity.

7. Paul's second "trustworthy saying" is this, "Whoever aspires to be an overseer desires a noble task."

   • Why is that desiring a noble (honorable, beautiful) task?

   • Read Mark 10:42-45. These are the instructions Jesus gave regarding leadership roles in His kingdom. We call this servant-leadership. Keep this in mind throughout this lesson.

8. Read 1 Timothy 3:1-7. List the qualifications for an elder in the chart below. Then, read Titus 1:6-9 and do the same. Notice the similarities.

   1 Timothy 3:1-7   **Titus 1:6-9**

Scriptural Insight: When you look at the qualifications for an elder in both letters, you see that the qualification words are masculine in gender, indicating elders are to be male. The office of deacon included both male and female (v. 11). That is consistent with God's activity in the Old Testament. Since creation, men have been responsible for the spiritual welfare of God's people (Genesis 18:19). Regarding the religious worship of Israel under the Mosaic Law, only males of the tribe of Levi and the clan of Aaron served as priests. God excluded other males, and all females, from the priesthood. Though a few women served as civil rulers in Israel (e.g., Deborah), there is no record of a female priest or a female high priest. (*Dr. Constable's Notes on 1 Timothy 2020 Edition,* pp. 133, 139)
Note: To see how women served their worship communities in other ways, see the "Scriptural Insight" in Lesson 3 Day Four Study.

9. Were you surprised that these qualifications focus primarily on character qualities (godliness) rather than abilities or status in society? How do these qualifications fit Jesus' instructions for His followers (Mark 10:42-45) when they are put in positions of leadership?

Focus on the Meaning: The main qualifications are mature character demonstrated over time. Spiritual leaders are not "picked." They are identified by others watching. The Bible doesn't describe how the elders are to govern. Each church is free to choose its own form. The importance is in the character of the men who are holding office.

10. How do biblical qualifications for servant-leadership compare to what you know the world in general considers as qualifications for leadership?

11. Regarding 1 Timothy 3:6, why would giving a recent or new convert a leadership role in the church not be a good thing …

- for him?

- for the church?

Focus on the Meaning: How new? There should be evidence that he can function as an elder (teaching, leading, defending the faith, etc.) without becoming "conceited." Inherent in the idea of "conceit" is the notion of being "blinded" or "beclouded."... So the church should guard new converts from it by keeping them back from premature appointment as elders. (*Dr. Constable's Notes on 1 Timothy 2020 Edition,* p. 72)

12. Why is an elder having a good reputation with outsiders essential for him and for the church?

13. ***Deeper Discoveries (optional):*** Read the following verses to glean some of the responsibilities of the elders of a New Testament church. Acts 20:28-31; Hebrews 13:7, 17; 1 Thessalonians 5:12; 1 Timothy 5:17; Titus 1:9; and James 5:14.

What application will you make to adorn yourself with godliness?

14. Consider the leadership roles you currently have in the many areas of your life (family, community, work, church etc.). Look at the list of leadership qualifications we just studied. Which character qualities do you want to cultivate or deepen in your life? What specific steps will you take to do so? Pray that God will work in your life to help you develop the character qualities you need to be a servant-leader to those you are leading.

Respond to the Lord about what you learned today.

DAY THREE STUDY

Read 1 Timothy 3:1-16. Ask the Lord Jesus to teach you through His Word.

Today, we will focus on vv. 8-13, the office of deacon.

What does it mean?

> **From the Greek:** "Deacon" (Gr. *diakonos*, v. 8; lit. "servant") is a word the New Testament writers used frequently. In time, the churches recognized official servants of the churches, and these people held office as "deacons."

The office of deacon is separate from the office of elder and open to both men and women as described in the text and seen elsewhere in the New Testament.

15. Like elders, Paul states that deacons must also possess certain leadership qualifications. In the space below, list the qualifications for the male deacons that Paul discussed in vv. 8-10 & 12. (We'll address vs. 11 separately.)

Paul addressed the qualifications for female deacons in v. 11. He started out with "in the same way" referring to what is expected of the male deacons. This would include holding to the deep truths of the faith with a clear conscience. Notice that the words are very similar to those used by Paul in v. 8. Read the "Scriptural Insight" below.

> **Scriptural Insight:** The Greek word translated "women" in vs. 11 refers to any woman—whether married, single, or widowed. It is a term of respect. The same Greek word for deacon, *diakonos*, is used of Phoebe in Romans 16:1, where it is translated as servant. The description in 1 Timothy 3:11 could be referring to female deacons. It is unlikely to be the wives of deacons since the wives of elders, a more influential office, are not addressed, either in 1 Timothy or Titus. Early Church writings have numerous allusions to women serving the church. Some taught other women due to the strict separation of the sexes or served the church body as the widows addressed in 1 Timothy 5.

16. What character qualities should female candidates for deacon possess (1 Timothy 3:11)?

17. Since the descriptions are specifically addressed to women, let's consider their meanings and importance. Consider what each word or phrase means and would look like in someone's life. Then, consider why that would be important for anyone to have who is in a servant-leader position in the church.

Character quality	What it would look like	Why it is important for leaders
Worthy of respect (honorable)—		
Not malicious talkers (not slanderers)—		
Temperate (sober, not addicted to wine or similar)—		
Trustworthy in everything (faithful)—		

Focus on the Meaning: No higher compliment can be paid to a Christian than to call [her] a godly person. [She] might be a conscientious parent, a zealous church worker, a dynamic spokesman for Christ, or a talented Christian leader; but none of these things matters if, at the same time, [she] is not a godly person. (Jerry Bridges, *The Practice of Godliness*)

18. ***Deeper Discoveries (optional):*** What is the role of a deacon? Whereas the elder office apparently arose out of Jewish religious life, the deacon office seems to have developed from an incident in the early history of the church (i.e., Acts 6:1-6). Read Acts 6:1-6 for the prototype of what later became the "office" of deacon in the church.

Historical Insight: In Greek society, the *diakonos* (servant) was one who gave lowly service, an act that was not considered dignified in a culture that valued ruling instead. But, Jesus reversed this evaluation (Luke 22:27; Mark 10:43-45).

19. What differences do you see in 1 Timothy 3:1-12 between the leadership **qualifications** for elders and for deacons?

20. Concerning both elders (vv. 4-5) and deacons (v. 12), managing one's family well is listed as a qualification for leadership for both offices. In that culture, men and women were expected to marry and have children. If someone has a family, why would this be an important consideration for leadership?

Think About It: The family is a training class and proving ground for leaders in the church. We can determine much about an individual's fitness to lead in church by finding out how he or she behaves at home. How we behave at home tells others much about our character and conduct. Our spouse, children, and relatives can provide feedback and encouragement to improve our character and conduct. Home is a proving ground because we must demonstrate the skills for leading the church by effectively leading our own families. Because the church is God's family, those who set their hearts on leadership should start at home. Those who are heavily involved in the church should never neglect their family responsibilities. *(Life Application Study Bible)*

21. What is the reward for serving well as a servant-leader in Christ's church (v. 13)?

What application will you make to adorn yourself with godliness?

22. The character qualities listed for women in 1 Timothy 3:11 are not just good for leaders but are also evidence of godliness in a woman's life. As you adorn yourself with godliness, you will want to adorn yourself with these.

    • *Worthy of respect (honorable):* A woman worthy of respect is recognized by her devotion to God and willingness to submit to the authority structures in her life, including the authority of Scripture. Do you desire this in your life? Ask the Lord Jesus to show you how to be a woman devoted to God who is worthy of respect.

- *Not malicious talkers (slanderers):* A woman worthy of respect remembers to not share sensitive information (personal and confidential) in inappropriate settings (to those who don't need to know). Every Christian woman should use discretion when talking about people so as not to mar another believer's reputation. Read Ephesians 4:29 to see the positive way to use your gift of speech. Do you desire this in your life? Ask the Lord Jesus to show you how to not use your gift of speech to talk maliciously about someone or slander them but to encourage and build them up instead.

- *Temperate (sober, not addicted to wine or similar excess):* A woman worthy of respect yields to the Holy Spirit's control of her behavior, attitude, and emotions more than the control of any substance, emotions, or personal preferences. Do you desire this? Ask the Lord Jesus to help you overcome any addictions you have to whatever is currently controlling you more than the Holy Spirit.

- *Trustworthy in everything (faithful):* A woman worthy of respect is reliable in doing what she's been asked to do. She is also diligent in pursuing and abiding in biblical truth. Do you desire this? Ask the Lord Jesus to help you be faithful to Him in everything. But, every Christian woman should be devoted to God and to do what God asks of her.

DAY FOUR STUDY

Read 1 Timothy 3:1-16. Ask the Lord Jesus to teach you through His Word.

Today, we will focus on vv. 14-16.

What does it mean?

23. Focus on v. 15. This was a view of the church that was foundational to all Paul's instructions in this letter. Note: the local church building is not the "house of God" as the temple was in Jewish times. It is just a building until the people of God are in it. The community of believers is the location of God's presence on earth, not any building.

- How did Paul describe the church?

- What does each word picture convey about the church?

- Why is it important for you to understand your local church in this way?

> **Think About It:** The local church is a family (or "household") of believers (cf. 5:1-2). It should, therefore, conduct its corporate life as a family—rather than as a business, a country club, an entertainment center, a military group, or some other organization. (*Dr. Constable's Notes on 1 Timothy 2020 Edition,* p. 79)

24. ***Deeper Discoveries (optional):*** Do a search on other metaphors the New Testament uses to describe the church. See Ephesians 2 and 1 Corinthians 12.

25. In 1 Timothy 3:16, the mystery from which true godliness springs is Christ. Jesus' life and ministry clarified this "mystery" by showing what "godliness" looks like (John 14:9). Paul described Christ with words that may have been a hymn or creed used by the church. In the space below, write these beautiful words about Christ. Put an "Amen" at the end!

What application will you make to adorn yourself with godliness?

26. Do you consider your local church as Paul did—as a household of faith serving the living God rather than as a corporation, country club, or entertainment center? Ask the Lord to show you where you might be thinking of your church in the wrong way and how to correct that.

27. In Lesson Four, we saw several evidences or examples of godliness. I've just chosen a few to put in the chart. Feel free to add to the list in the chart below. Choose one godly character quality or behavior from this passage. Ask the Lord Jesus to give you a desire for that in your life and to adorn you with that. He has the power to make it happen.

Verse(s)	What godliness looks like
v. 8	Pursuing honest gain rather than dishonest gain
v. 9	Keeping hold of the deep truths of the faith with a clear conscience
v. 11	Being a woman worthy of respect
v. 11	Using words about others in a kind and truthful way
v. 11	Being sober with respect to wine or other addictions
v. 11	Being trustworthy in everything you are given to do
v. 15	Viewing the local church as the household of the living God

Respond to the Lord about what you learned today.

Recommended: Listen to the podcast "A Godly Woman Is Worthy of Respect" after doing this lesson to reinforce what you have learned. Use the following listener guide.

A Godly Woman Is Worthy of Respect

- Every church needs godly women leaders. And women readily respond to the needs of the church. Wise male leaders recognize this and encourage the women in their churches to serve as the Lord has gifted them.

- Because of Jesus' example and the truth He taught, women were prominent in the activities of the New Testament Church. In Acts alone, 33 women are named specifically. Many hosted church meetings in their homes. Priscilla actively participated in a church teaching ministry alongside her husband. Dorcas helped widows and the poor, using her sewing skills. In Romans 16, Paul referred to 4 women in terms not used for the men. He said that they "worked hard in the Lord," an expression that in the Greek means "toiling to the point of exhaustion."

IDENTIFYING LEADERS

- Identifying leaders takes time and observation. And, none of the qualifications for leadership have anything to do with physical beauty or social status.

  "In the same way, the women are to be worthy of respect, not malicious talkers but temperate and trustworthy in everything." (1 Timothy 3:11)

- Having the right character qualities doesn't mean that someone will be a great small group leader. But, women with those characteristics have adorned themselves with godliness and are good role models for other women in their groups. All Christian women should aspire to have those same descriptions attached to their names.

BEING A WOMAN WORTHY OF RESPECT

- A woman worthy of respect is recognized by her devotion to God and willingness to submit to the authority structures in her life, including the authority of Scripture. Then, how she lives out that devotion to God is recognized in her character. She adorns herself with godliness more often than ungodliness.

- When it comes to identifying leaders for a particular ministry, these are the questions we considered for our Bible Study small groups:
  - ✓ Is she respected by other ministry leaders for who she is and how she behaves?
  - ✓ Is she more interested in the goals of the ministry than in her own agenda?
  - ✓ Is she submissive to authority? Can she follow the proper procedure for dealing with issues by going through the biblical authority structure for the church body?

- If the answer is yes to those questions, she fits the description of being a woman worthy of respect.

A WOMAN WORTHY OF RESPECT IS NOT A MALICIOUS TALKER.

- A malicious talker speaks false accusations to slander someone and damage their reputation.

- Instead, we should avoid such rotten talk and speak that which is beneficial for building up the one who is listening or reading. *Ephesians 4:29*

- A woman worthy of respect remembers to not share sensitive information (personal and confidential) in inappropriate settings (to those who don't need to know). Only share on a "need to know" basis and keep confidences.

- Women in the church need to use discernment about sharing information that may sound critical or complaining. If you have a concern about any ministry or another leader, you need to talk to the person who is part of the decision-making process. Then, trust your leadership and give them time to work on it. While waiting, you can pray for God to guide them.

A WOMAN WORTHY OF RESPECT IS A TEMPERATE WOMAN.

- To be "temperate" means to be sober, to abstain from wine either entirely or at least from excess. The first thought would be excess in the way of addiction to alcohol. But, excess can apply to anything we use habitually to cope with life.

- Anything that controls you more than the Spirit of God can be an intoxicant and draw you away from devotion to Christ and living a life that pleases Him. But, our God, who can free us from the bondage to sin and death, can free us from this as well.

- To be temperate can also mean to be well-balanced. A woman is well-balanced when she holds on to the truth of God's Word and doesn't let her emotions rule over her.

A WOMAN WORTHY OF RESPECT IS TRUSTWORTHY IN EVERYTHING.

- Being "trustworthy" means faithfulness in the transaction of business, the execution of commands, or the discharge of official duties. It involves doing what you've been asked to do and doing it the way you've been asked to do it, assuming it's biblical.

- Being trustworthy also refers to someone who trusts in God and His promises and is living dependently on Him more than on herself. When someone needs help, you point her to God and His Word so she can rely on Him first more than relying on you.

Women were given equality in the church and were given responsibility for leadership where before they had very little. Christianity elevated women to their very best back then and still does today. May we be the kind of women that someone in our world might exclaim, "What women these Christians have!" A woman adorned with godliness is worthy of such respect.

Let Jesus satisfy your heart with such love for God that you will want to live a life that pleases Him.

5: Desiring to Look Your Best

1 Timothy 4:1-16

DAY ONE STUDY—GET THE BIG PICTURE

Ask the Lord Jesus to teach you through His Word.

What does the Bible say?

Read the Bible passage below (NIV) including verses from the last lesson. Use your own method (colored pencils, lines, shapes) to mark 1) anything that grabs your attention, 2) words you want to understand, and 3) topics you have seen before in this letter. Draw arrows between thoughts that connect. Put a star ✱ next to anything you think relates to godliness.

3 *[14] Although I hope to come to you soon, I am writing you these instructions so that, [15] if I am delayed, you will know how people ought to conduct themselves in God's household, which is the church of the living God, the pillar and foundation of the truth. [16] Beyond all question, the mystery from which true godliness springs is great:*

He appeared in the flesh, was vindicated by the Spirit, was seen by angels, was preached among the nations, was believed on in the world, was taken up in glory.

4 *[1] The Spirit clearly says that in later times some will abandon the faith and follow deceiving spirits and things taught by demons. [2] Such teachings come through hypocritical liars, whose consciences have been seared as with a hot iron. [3] They forbid people to marry and order them to abstain from certain foods, which God created to be received with thanksgiving by those who believe and who know the truth. [4] For everything God created is good, and nothing is to be rejected if it is received with thanksgiving, [5] because it is consecrated by the word of God and prayer.*

[6] If you point these things out to the brothers and sisters you will be a good minister of Christ Jesus, nourished on the truths of the faith and of the good teaching that you have followed. [7] Have nothing to do with godless myths and old wives' tales; rather, train yourself to be godly. [8] For physical training is of some value, but godliness has value for all things, holding promise for both the present life and the life to come. [9] This is a trustworthy saying that deserves full acceptance. [10] That is why we labor and strive, because we have put our hope in the living God, who is the Savior of all people, and especially of those who believe.

[11] Command and teach these things. [12] Don't let anyone look down on you because you are young, but set an example for the believers in speech, in conduct, in love, in faith and in purity. [13] Until I come, devote yourself to the public reading of Scripture, to preaching and to teaching. [14] Do not neglect your gift, which was given you through prophecy when the body of elders laid their hands on you.

[15] Be diligent in these matters; give yourself wholly to them, so that everyone may see your progress. [16] Watch your life and doctrine closely. Persevere in them, because if you do, you will save both yourself and your hearers.

1. What grabbed your attention from 1 Timothy 4:1-16?

2. What verses or specific words do you want to understand better?

3. What words or phrases are repeated in this passage? Give verses.

4. What topics (if any) in this passage have we studied in previous lessons? Give verses.

5. What verses illustrate or help you understand what godliness looks like?

6. *Adorn yourself with godliness:* From this lesson's passage (1 Timothy 4:1-16), choose one verse to dwell upon all week long. Write it in the space below. Ask God to teach you through this verse.

Respond to the Lord about what you learned today.

DAY TWO STUDY

Read 1 Timothy 4:1-16. Ask the Lord Jesus to teach you through His Word.

We will focus on vv. 1-6 in this session.

What does it say?

7. Answer the following questions based on what is written in the text.

    In the later times, some will do what (v. 1)?

    Such teachings come through _____, whose consciences have

    been _____ (v. 2).

    Those false teachers teach what (v. 3, first part)?

    God created food to be what (v. 3, second part)?

    For everything God created is good, and should be received how (4)?

    Why can we receive all kinds of food with thanksgiving (5)?

    Pointing these truths out to the brothers and sisters will show Timothy to be what (v. 6)?

> **Focus on the Meaning:** "Consecrated" means to make or declare set apart to the
> service of God, to dedicate to some purpose.

What does it mean?

> **Scriptural Insight:** "In later times" does not refer to the end times but to the whole
> time between the two advents of Jesus.... God had revealed through Christ that, as
> time passed, some who held the truth would repudiate it (Matt. 13:21; 24:10-11; Mark
> 4:17; 13:22; Luke 8:13). (*Dr. Constable's Notes on 1 Timothy 2020 Edition,* p. 83)

8. Whether those abandoning the faith are true Christians or those just professing to be
    Christians is unclear in the text. It is possible for Christians to grow lukewarm or cold in their
    devotion to God and His truth (Revelation 3:15-16). This does not mean, however, that they

will lose their salvation, since salvation is God's work, not ours. The results of their behavior, however, are the same.

- Some abandoned the faith to follow deceiving spirits (v. 1). Besides what is given in vv. 2-3, review 1 Timothy 1:3-7 to see the other deceptions being taught.

- Verse 2 literally says that the teachings come from "the hypocrisy of liars seared in their own consciences as with a branding iron." What could this mean? What would it look like to have a seared conscience?

Focus on the Meaning: They refused to respond to the truth that they knew. Now they called lies "the truth," and that is "hypocrisy." The lies were related to ... the idea that abstinence from physical things is essential for spiritual purity (see Colossians 2:20-23). Specifically, those teachers forbade "marriage" and the eating of some "foods." The latter could also be the influence of Jewish legalism. There may be physical reasons for not eating certain foods. Likewise, there may be physical reasons why in individual cases marrying may not be wise or desirable. Nevertheless, God has approved the institution of marriage. (*Dr. Constable's Notes on 1 Timothy 2020 Edition*, pp. 84-85)

In Mark chapter 13, Jesus warned His disciples 8 times to "watch out that no one deceives you," "be on guard," and "stay alert." A Christ-follower's greatest danger is not war, not calamity, not suffering, not persecution, and not even betrayal. It is deception (Mark 13:5). Deception feeds apostasy—an aggressive and positive revolt against God by so-called religious people. Apostasy is driven by people who may even call themselves "Christian" but are influential fakers who draw people away from Christ, especially when they claim to no longer believe in Him. We have a spiritual enemy, and deceiving us is one of his best means for making us ineffective at pursuing Christ completely. Deception is always undermined by demons (1 Timothy 4:1).

9. Read the following verses to see what identifies such influential fakers and the harm they do.

- 2 Corinthians 11:3-4, 13-14—

- 2 Timothy 4:3-4—

Think About It: What about professing Christians on the public stage (authors, worship singers, actors) who claim they no longer believe today? That seems to happen on a regular basis. Only God knows their true natures, whether believers or not. If they are true Christians, the Holy Spirit will work on their hearts to bring them back to the Lord. If they are not true Christians, they fit the descriptions you read about in the verses above.

10. According to 1 Timothy 4:6, on what should we nourish our faith?

What application will you make to adorn yourself with godliness?

11. In 2 Timothy 4:3-4, Paul warned about a process by which we can become willing participants in our own deception. We can do something about such falling away from truth in our own lives and in those within our spheres of influence.

    - How do you see what Paul described in both 1 Timothy 4:1-3 and 2 Timothy 4:3-4 taking place in our world? Do you personally know anyone like those described? How will you pray for them specifically?

    - Was this ever a portrait of you? If so, how have you changed? To what do you attribute this change?

    - Are you being constantly nourished on the truths of the faith? Or, do you find yourself sporadically eating the good food of God's Word with lots of junk food of the world in between?

    - Are you careful to critically analyze what you see, read, and hear? How do you know if it is biblical truth or not?

12. Consider those professing Christians on today's public stage (authors, worship singers, actors) who claim they no longer believe. These modern-day influencers are often praised in social media for having the courage to publicly express their doubts and renounce their faith/belief system. How can we as believers respond to this in such a way as to promote honest discussion about their doubts while continuing to stand firm in the truth of God's Word?

Respond to the Lord about what you learned today.

DAY THREE STUDY

Read 1 Timothy 4:1-16. Ask the Lord Jesus to teach you through His Word.

We will focus on vv. 7-10 in this session.

What does it mean?

13. Read v. 7 in several translations.

   • What are we to avoid?

   • In the context of this chapter and 1 Timothy 1:3-7, what could that mean?

Focus on the Meaning: Paul told Timothy to have nothing to do with worldly fables (NAS). A worldly fable is worldly reasoning about why something happens and what you should do about it or to keep it from happening again. Paul's advice is perfect for us today as well.

The phrase "old wives' tales" comes from the KJV of the Bible. Paul called these tales *graōdeis*, which literally means "old womanish," a word associated with superstition, silliness, and gossip. He could have been ridiculing the "endless myths and genealogies" of the false teachers (1:4). This is the only place in the Bible where that word is used.

14. Write verse 8 in the space below. This is Paul's third "trustworthy statement" in this letter.

Focus on the Meaning: Paul introduced an athletic image with the words "train yourself." The verb here is *gymnaze*, from which comes the English "gymnasium." Paul often used athletic analogies to drive home the need for spiritual discipline. "Physical training" is *gymnasia*, "exercise," used only here in the New Testament. (*The Bible Knowledge Commentary New Testament,* p. 740)

15. We are to pursue godliness. The word "pursue" indicates unrelenting, persevering effort. Paul encouraged Timothy to pursue godliness (the goal) through training (the means). One of the rewards for this training is being able to avoid the dangers shown in 1 Timothy 4:1-3.

   • What would be included in training for godliness? Consider what you have learned so far.

   • Read 2 Peter 1:3. Why is godliness achievable?

- Why is training for godliness of greater value than physical training?

Think About It: It is both the privilege and duty of every Christian to pursue godliness, to train [herself] to be godly, to study diligently the practice of godliness. We don't need any special talent or equipment. God has given to each one of us "everything we need for life and godliness" (2 Peter 1:3). The most ordinary Christian has all that he needs, and the most talented Christian must use those same means in the practice of godliness. A godly life is not wearisome, but this is true only because a godly person is first of all devoted to God. (Jerry Bridges, *The Practice of Godliness*)

16. According to 1 Timothy 4:10, why was Paul willing to labor and strive in the pursuit of godliness? Note: This is the devotion to God part of godliness.

Focus on the Meaning: What is hope? Your answer depends on your perspective. The kind of hope that the world offers is generally the wishful thinking kind where someone is not sure they will get what they want or need but "hopes" they will. Biblical hope is the confident expectation that God will fulfill His promises to you because your hope is based on the character and faithfulness of God. We can have this hope because we have faith in Christ. Christ is the Savior of all men (v. 10), but only those who believe will be saved (see John 3:16; 1 John 2:2) and can have this hope.

What application will you make to adorn yourself with godliness?

17. Paul described his work to pursue godliness in verse 10 as laboring and striving to pursue godliness.

From the Greek: The Greek term translated *strive* means to strive as in a contest for a prize, straining every nerve to attain to the object (Luke 13:24); to put forth every effort, involving toil, (Colossians 1:29; 1 Timothy 4:10). (*Vines Expository Dictionary of New Testament Words*)

- For which do you strive more readily—to pursue physical training or to train yourself to be godly? Why?

- If you have trusted in Christ for your salvation, you have already begun the process of spiritual training that leads to godliness. That training begins with God's truth found in His word—believing it, knowing it to get to know God better, and obeying it to live a life that pleases Him. As Paul wrote in 1 Timothy 4:6, stay nourished in the truths of the faith and good teaching. With this in mind, what practical steps do you take or can you take to train yourself to be godly?

- If you neglect spiritual training, how does that become obvious in your life?

Respond to the Lord about what you learned today.

DAY FOUR STUDY

Read 1 Timothy 4:1-16. Ask the Lord Jesus to teach you through His Word.

We will focus on vv. 11-16 in this session.

What does it mean?

In v. 11, Paul wrote, "Command and teach (literally, keep on teaching) these things." This refers to everything he said in vv. 1-10. Timothy would have been about 30 when he received this letter. He had been through a lot of training and experiences with Paul. He was not inexperienced in ministry but also not as bold as Paul.

> **Focus on the Meaning:** The Greek word translated "youthfulness" (v. 12) described people up to 40 years of age. As a comparatively young man, Timothy may have felt reluctant to instruct the elders in the Ephesian congregation, who were probably older than he. Most people regarded older people with great respect in his culture. Paul promised that no one in the church would discredit his teaching ministry if he backed it up with a godly lifestyle. (*Dr. Constable's Notes on 1 Timothy 2020 Edition*, p. 91)

The instruction in v. 12 is not just for the young but also for all ages. Paul listed 5 areas in which we can show ourselves examples as Christians to others watching—speech, conduct, love, faith, and purity.

18. *Speech:* Read Ephesians 4:25, 29 and Colossians 3:8; 4:6. How can you set an example for other believers in your speech? Feel free to add other verses that help.

19. *Conduct:* Read Philippians 1:27 and 1 Thessalonians 2:4-6. How can you set an example for other believers in your conduct? Feel free to add other verses that help.

20. *Love:* Read 1 Corinthians 13:4-8 and 1 Peter 4:8. How can you set an example for other believers in your love? Feel free to add other verses that help.

21. *Faith:* Read 1 Timothy 1:18-19 and Hebrews 11:1, 6. How can you set an example for other believers in your faith? Feel free to add other verses that help.

22. *Purity:* The word purity includes both sexual purity and moral cleanness. Read 1 Thessalonians 4:3-8 and Ephesians 5:3-4. How can you set an example for other believers in your purity? Feel free to add other verses that help.

Think About It: Many of us who live in western cultures find ourselves in a sex-craved society. Movies, television shows, books, and other entertainment venues generally encourage sexual promiscuity and promise that such "freedom" will make you happy. When you choose to pursue purity, you can feel alone at times because you are counter-cultural.

23. Back to 1 Timothy 4. The rest of this chapter, vv. 13-16, are full of instruction for the active Christian, especially those in a servant-leadership position. Notice all the action verbs or phrases. and why?

   - What are Paul's instructions to Timothy in vv. 13-14?

   - What are Paul's instructions to Timothy in vv. 15-16?

   - Why should he be so intentional in his life and doctrine?

   Think About It: Paul knew we all need a role model, a picture of Christ that makes the heart, mind, and ways of Christ visible and tangible. To step into a role of leadership is essentially to state, "Follow me as I follow Christ." If people are going to follow us, our primary task is to lead ourselves well ... The first step toward leading yourself well is following well ... And if you are a Christ follower, the practice of following [Christ] well is fundamental to your identity and may be one of the greatest tests of your character. (Heather Zempel, *Community Is Messy*, pages 67-68)

24. ***Deeper Discoveries (optional):*** Every Christian is given a spiritual gift or gifts at the moment of salvation. A spiritual gift is a supernatural capacity for service to God in the Body of Christ (Romans 12:4-8; 1 Corinthians 12:4-12; and Ephesians 4:11-13). All believers receive the same gift of the Holy Spirit but individually receive spiritual gifts that differ, according to the will of God, to be used for the common good, especially in the local church.

   You can take a free spiritual gifts assessment at the following website: www.churchgrowth.org.

   What did you discover about yourself regarding your spiritual gift(s) and how they could benefit your ministry at your church?

What application will you make to adorn yourself with godliness?

25. In the gospels, we see that Jesus would connect with people and impart truth to them. You are His visible representative for others to see your progress in following Christ (v. 15). And, He has used His servants to reach you and model for you how to follow Him.

- Who are the earthly examples who demonstrate (or, in the past, have demonstrated) to you how to follow Christ?

- In whom are you consciously investing right now so that they would learn how to follow Christ by imitating you? What results have you seen in their lives?

26. Looking at the 5 areas of life in which you can set an example for others (v. 12),

- In which of those areas would you admit that you don't set a very good example? Ask the Lord Jesus to give you the desire to follow Him more closely in that area and teach you how to do it through His Word and the Spirit power inside of you.

- In our sex-craved world, what do you do to maintain your sexual purity, even if you are married? Not just in your actions but also in your thoughts. How do you evaluate movies, TV shows, and books that are recommended to you? What do you do when you find something you are watching or reading to be an ungodly influence on you?

Dependent Living: The progression from temptation to sin may look like this:
1) A received thought produces familiarity.
2) Continued pondering produces a loss of repugnance and, eventually, curiosity.
3) Desires, sometimes a total surprise, are generated to experiment.
4) Having tried the activity, the flesh (like a goat) can learn to like, and even grow dependent, on any sensual stimulus.
Conclusion: We never outgrow our need to depend 100% upon Jesus Christ. Recognizing this should lead us to have compassion on one another (Galatians 6:1) and to not take risks with sinful behavior. The most damaging or dangerous are the ones that blindside you with a desire you didn't even know you could have! So, protect yourself at all times through prayer, "Lord, protect me from myself!"

27. In Lesson Five, we saw several evidences of godliness displayed—devotion to God expressed in a life pleasing to Him. Feel free to add to the list in the chart below. Choose one example of godliness from this passage. Ask the Lord Jesus to give you a desire for that in your life and to adorn you with that. He has the power to make it happen.

Verse(s)	What godliness looks like
v. 4	*Receive what God has created with thanksgiving.*
v. 6	*Stay nourished on the truths of the faith and good teaching that support them.*
v. 7	*Train yourself to be godly and avoid godless traditions*
v. 10	*Set your hope in the living God not in anything else.*
v. 12	*Exhibit godly speech, conduct, love, steadfast faith, and moral purity.*
v. 14	*Use your spiritual gift for the good of the body of Christ.*
vv.15-16	*Be the visible example of following Christ that others will see and imitate.*

Respond to the Lord about what you learned today.

Recommended: Listen to the podcast "Legalism Is Not Godliness" after doing this lesson to reinforce what you have learned. Use the following listener guide.

Legalism Is Not Godliness

Why would a Christian who has tasted the goodness of the Lord abandon Him? There are several reasons. One of them we see in 1 Timothy 4 is the influence of legalism.

LEGALISM IS NOT GODLINESS.

- Legalism is a works-based way of approaching the Christian life. It is taking your faith in Christ and adding other things you must do or not do to gain acceptance from God and maintain that to keep your salvation. You can recognize it as "faith plus" good works or "faith plus" following church rules.

- Legalism is not what is clearly taught in the New Testament about what sin is and what living a life that pleases God looks like. It is those extra rules that some person or organization has decided you must follow to be a "good Christian" and for God to love you. *1 Timothy 4:3-5*

- Legalism makes you feel guilt and shame, not gratitude and joy.

THE HYPOCRISY OF LEGALISM

- Jesus pointed out legalism in the Pharisees who kept their bodies squeaky clean while treating fellow Jews like dirt (Mark 7:18-23). Cleanliness is not next to godliness. What they did was hypocrisy. Hypocrisy comes from the word for "actor." It's playing a role.

- Christians who make mistakes and repent of them before God are not hypocrites. No Christian is perfect in life—no matter how old or established in their faith.

- Hypocrites are those who are outwardly conforming to what looks good, but their hearts are not tender toward God. They claim to know God, but by their actions deny Him (Titus 1:16).

- God isn't interested in outward conformity. He wants your heart to be right with Him, and right behavior that He asks you to do should follow that. But, legalism breeds hypocrisy.

THE HOPELESSNESS OF LEGALISM

- Christians start out accepting the Gospel of God's grace by their faith alone. Then, someone comes along and says, "That's not enough. You have to follow these rules if you want to be spiritual and if you want to stay saved." But, the rules are constantly changing so you never know if you are saved or not.

- Maybe you started out accepting the gift of salvation by faith in Jesus as a free gift. But then you have been thrown into such a works-related way of living this Christian life in order to maintain your acceptance before God. The result is that you stray away from enjoying a love-based relationship with Jesus to practicing a works-based religion.

- Outward performance is not godliness. But, the emphasis on "getting it right" with God can lead to hopelessness because no one can ever be able to ever please God enough. That leads someone to stop trying altogether and just give up.

WHY DOES LEGALISM PERSIST IN THE CHURCH TODAY?

- Why would someone think it necessary to create additional laws for Christians to follow? Often, it is the tendency to think that you can control sin through lots of rules.

- Legalism is used to motivate people to obedience by fear of punishment. It becomes a substitute for devotion to Christ.

GOD'S PLAN IS FOR YOU TO LIVE BY GRACE.

> *"For it is by grace you have been saved, through faith—and this is not from yourselves, it is the gift of God—**not by works**, so that no one can boast." (Ephesians 2:8-9)*

- Grace means "undeserved favor." God gives His favor to someone not because they are good enough to deserve it but because **His love chooses to do so**. We all receive this grace when we trust in Jesus.

- God wants you to relate to Him now on the basis of **His grace**. Jesus paid the complete price for you to be set free from your sinful past. You can do nothing more to make yourself acceptable to God.

- Paul understood those who had been relating to God through outward performance. God's overflowing grace sets you free from whatever has you in bondage—sin, guilt, religious expectations, whatever. *1 Timothy 1:13-14*

GRACE MOTIVATES YOU TO OBEDIENCE BY LOVE AND GRATITUDE FOR WHAT CHRIST HAS DONE.

- Knowing what Christ has done for you should motivate you by love and gratitude to live the kind of life that pleases God. You pursue godliness—godlikeness—because you love Him and are thankful for what He has done for you. You can freely accept that you are in Christ, a child of God, one of His saints, totally forgiven, accepted and loved by God. You can freely make that choice to serve Him wholeheartedly, without obligation or fear.

- Consider how any "faith plus something else" teaching has affected your life, emotions, thinking, or relationship with God and others. Then, let it go and cling to the truth of your identity in Christ. Don't let legalism rob you of your relationship with God.

Let Jesus satisfy your heart with such love for God that you will want to live a life that pleases Him.

6: Clothing Relationships with Respect

1 Timothy 5:1-16

DAY ONE STUDY—GET THE BIG PICTURE

Ask the Lord Jesus to teach you through His Word.

What does the Bible say?

Read the Bible passage below (NIV) including verses from the last lesson. Use your own method (colored pencils, lines, shapes) to mark 1) anything that grabs your attention, 2) words you want to understand, and 3) topics you have seen before in this letter. Draw arrows between thoughts that connect. Put a star ✱ next to anything you think relates to godliness.

4 *¹¹ Command and teach these things. ¹² Don't let anyone look down on you because you are young, but set an example for the believers in speech, in conduct, in love, in faith and in purity. ¹³ Until I come, devote yourself to the public reading of Scripture, to preaching and to teaching. ¹⁴ Do not neglect your gift, which was given you through prophecy when the body of elders laid their hands on you. ¹⁵ Be diligent in these matters; give yourself wholly to them, so that everyone may see your progress. ¹⁶ Watch your life and doctrine closely. Persevere in them, because if you do, you will save both yourself and your hearers.*

5 *¹ Do not rebuke an older man harshly, but exhort him as if he were your father. Treat younger men as brothers, ² older women as mothers, and younger women as sisters, with absolute purity.*

³ Give proper recognition to those widows who are really in need. ⁴ But if a widow has children or grandchildren, these should learn first of all to put their religion into practice by caring for their own family and so repaying their parents and grandparents, for this is pleasing to God. ⁵ The widow who is really in need and left all alone puts her hope in God and continues night and day to pray and to ask God for help. ⁶ But the widow who lives for pleasure is dead even while she lives. ⁷ Give the people these instructions, so that no one may be open to blame. ⁸ Anyone who does not provide for their relatives, and especially for their own household, has denied the faith and is worse than an unbeliever.

⁹ No widow may be put on the list of widows unless she is over sixty, has been faithful to her husband, ¹⁰ and is well known for her good deeds, such as bringing up children, showing hospitality, washing the feet of the Lord's people, helping those in trouble and devoting herself to all kinds of good deeds.

¹¹ As for younger widows, do not put them on such a list. For when their sensual desires overcome their dedication to Christ, they want to marry. ¹² Thus they bring judgment on themselves, because they have broken their first pledge. ¹³ Besides, they get into the habit of being idle and going about from house to house. And not only do they become idlers, but also busybodies who talk nonsense, saying things they ought not to. ¹⁴ So I counsel younger widows to marry, to have children, to manage their homes and to give the enemy no opportunity for slander. ¹⁵ Some have in fact already turned away to follow Satan.

¹⁶ If any woman who is a believer has widows in her care, she should continue to help them and not let the church be burdened with them, so that the church can help those widows who are really in need.

1. What grabbed your attention from 1 Timothy 5:1-16?

2. What verses or specific words do you want to understand better?

3. What words or phrases are repeated in this passage? Give verses.

4. What topics (if any) in this passage have we studied in previous lessons? Give verses.

5. What verses illustrate or help you understand what godliness looks like?

6. ***Adorn yourself with godliness:*** From this lesson's passage (1 Timothy 5:1-16), choose one verse to dwell upon all week long. Write it in the space below. Ask God to teach you through this verse.

Respond to the Lord about what you learned today.

DAY TWO STUDY

Read 1 Timothy 5:1-16. Ask the Lord Jesus to teach you through His Word.

We will focus on vv. 1-8 and v. 16 in this session.

One of the benefits of studying 1 Timothy and Titus together is seeing the volume of information written to and about women in them—more than any other epistles. In these letters are references to women as believers and disciples. In 1 Timothy 2, Paul encouraged women to take advantage of the privilege of being educated in the truths of the Christian faith and to do so with a willingness to listen and submit to that good teaching. In 1 Timothy 3, we read the desired character qualities for the women who served the church doing the work of a deacon (servant-leader). Christian discipleship develops those character qualities, enabling a woman to serve someone else. And now here in 1 Timothy 5, we see women who are ministering to others.

Want to know what a godly woman looks like? It's in 1 Timothy. Want to know what a woman who is not godly looks like? It's in here as well. No guessing about what our Heavenly Father wants for His daughters. There are more references in Titus. In fact, you could highlight all the passages giving instruction strictly to and about women in these two letters plus 2 Timothy and have a nice pattern to follow or avoid.

What does it mean?

Looking at verses 1-2, we find more instruction to Timothy (and us). This time the topic is how to deal with those around us (of all ages) when the need for correction arises. Remember the local church is a family (or "household") of believers (1 Timothy 3:15).

7. How should a pastor or ministry leader act toward various members of the "family?"

   - Older men—

   - Younger men—

   - Older women—

   - Younger women—

The next passage takes on a subject that is given more verses than any other topic thus far in the letter—helping women in need.

> **Focus on the Meaning:** The Greek word translated as "widow" (v. 3) certainly includes a woman whose husband has died. But in Paul's context, the word "widow" was also used to describe a woman who was mate-less—a "without-a-man woman." According to the Jewish philosopher Philo (25 BC–AD 50), a "widow" was an older unmarried woman. This use of "widow" also shows up in the church fathers where women who never married were called widows. (Dr. Sandra Glahn, *"Can a Woman Be a Pastor? Looking at the New Testament"* accessed on Bible.org)

8. Focusing on vv. 3-4: The goal of the instructions that follow v. 3 is to determine which widows should receive specific help from the church.

   - What would determine those women who were really in need (vv. 4, 5, 16)?

- What does Paul say about a needy woman who has children or grandchildren (vv. 4, 16)?

> **Historical Insight:** In Acts 6, the church had established a charitable outreach to widows. Now 30 years later the ministry to the many widows in the culture showed signs of being a major burden to the congregation. Paul was therefore eager in this passage to identify those who did not truly need help in order to leave enough for those who did. And, in a world with no nurses or nursing homes, the most natural person to bathe and feed an infirm matron would have been her daughter, granddaughter, and/or daughter-in-law.

9. Widows are women first. Remember that our definition of godliness is a devotion to God expressed in a life that is pleasing to Him. In light of that …

- What did Paul mean when he identified the woman who "puts her hope in God?"

- Compare the woman described in v. 5 with the woman described in v. 6. What is different?

> **Focus on the Meaning:** Because the widow in v. 6 mentioned is even included in this discussion, she must be part of the church fellowship and, therefore, a believer. When Paul said that she is dead even while she lives, the word he used for dead can mean to be useless. He used a different word for those who are spiritually dead or dead in sin. The widow of v. 6 may be saved but useless to the Lord's work.

10. *Deeper Discoveries (optional):*

- Research the plight of widows in the Roman Empire to get a better understanding of their situation. What were their options?

- Regarding Jewish widows, they were considered to be under God's special care. They wore distinctive garb so they could be identified. Read Exodus 22:22-23, Deuteronomy 14:28-29; and 24:19-22. How did God plan for the community to provide for widows and orphans?

- How does your culture provide for elderly widows?

11. According to 1 Timothy 5:7, why should they provide (literally, "to think beforehand") for such needy women in the congregation?

12. Paul said that any Christian (male or female) who does not provide for their own family members has "denied the faith and is worse than an unbeliever."

- How might a believer be considered "worse than an unbeliever" in this situation?

- How does providing for your own family members relate to godliness? Note: "Learn to put their religion into practice (v. 4, NIV)" literally means "learn to show godliness."

What application will you make to adorn yourself with godliness?

> **Scriptural Insight:** One of the values of Scripture is that it has an answer to every human problem, of whatever kind, era, dimension or significance. It is true that not all church problems of 62 A.D. are the identical problems of the church two thousand years later. But even in such instances, timeless principles can be derived from the Bible account and applied to any succeeding generation. (Irving L. Jensen, *1&2 Timothy and Titus, A Self-study Guide*)

13. In today's society,

- Whom would we consider to be "widows who are really in need" in our churches? What do they need besides material provisions?

- Read James 1:27 and Romans 12:13. As followers of Christ, what does God expect of us as women in our homes, church, and community to help the needy? How are you doing this?

Respond to the Lord about what you learned today.

DAY THREE STUDY

Read 1 Timothy 5:1-16. Ask the Lord Jesus to teach you through His Word.

We will focus on vv. 9-10 in this session.

What does it mean?

> **Historical Insight:** What was the list mentioned in 1 Timothy 5:9 and 11? The words refer to being enrolled in a group such as soldiers enlisted in the army. Early Christian writers mentioned such a group of women who took a pledge (1 Timothy 5:12) to serve Christ and His church. They were respected as the elders were respected. They were overseers over the rest of the women. And, they had charge of the other widows and orphans supported by the church. This is Women's Ministry in action. The early Church considered ministry to women by women as very important. They had a specific task to fill for the local church.

14. From verses 5 and 9-10, list the qualifications for a widow to be put "on the list" to qualify for assistance from the church. Note: The "faithful to her husband" (if she had been married) parallels the qualifications for the elders and deacons in 1 Timothy 3.

> **Historical Insight:** Why 60 years old? At this age, most widows probably became incapable of providing for their own needs, and most would no longer have the opportunity to remarry. And, sixty was the recognized age in antiquity when one became an 'old' man or woman. (*Dr. Constable's Notes on 1 Timothy 2020 Edition*, p. 102)

15. ***Deeper Discoveries (optional):*** Although our western culture places a lot of emphasis on youth and trying to stay young, growing older does not mean no longer having a place in the family of God. Read Psalm 92:12-15. What do these verses tell us about God and our relationship to Him as we grow older? What should be the aim for anyone growing older? Is this your aim?

The woman over 60 who qualified for receiving financial help from the church should be "well known for her good deeds." This should be the goal of all Christian women. Since behavior is living out what is inside, good deeds are a natural extension of adorning yourself with godliness. Good deeds don't save us. Good deeds are how we live out our life in Christ, letting Him live His life through us. This is pleasing to God (v. 7).

16. Why is doing good deeds held in such high regard? Consider what you have learned so far in 1 Timothy. Also, look at 1 Timothy 6:19.

> **Think About It:** The church, which is invisible, made up of all believers who are in the body of Christ, *manifests* itself down here upon the earth in local assemblies, in the local churches. Now, just to put a steeple on a building and a bell in the steeple and a pulpit down front and a choir in the loft singing the doxology doesn't mean it is a local church in the New Testament sense of the word. There must be certain identifying features. .... In all three epistles [1 Timothy, Titus, and 2 Timothy] Paul is dealing with two things: the *creed* of the church and the *conduct* of the church. For the church within, the worship must be right. For the church outside, good works must be manifested. (J. Vernon McGee, *Thru-the-Bible Commentary Series*)

The Bible tells all of us women who profess to worship God that we should adorn ourselves with good deeds (1 Timothy 2:9-10). Through Paul's writing in 1 Timothy 5:10, the Holy Spirit gave us four examples of good works for women adorned with godliness. Let's consider these more closely.

17. *Bringing up children:* In our career-driven society, we sometimes need to be reminded of the value of bringing up children—whether a woman's own children or the children of other women. What would be involved in bringing up children? Why would bringing up (or influencing) children be considered a good work by a woman adorned with godliness?

18. *Showing hospitality:* What would be involved in showing hospitality? Why would this be considered a good deed by a woman adorned with godliness?

19. *Washing the feet of the Lord's people:* If you look back at John 13:5-17, Jesus illustrated what it looks like to serve one another in a humble fashion. "Washing the saints' feet" became a figure of speech for humble service in the church family. What would that include? Why would this be considered a good deed by a woman adorned with godliness?

20. *Helping those in trouble:* What would fall in the category of helping those in distress? Why would helping those in trouble or distress be considered a good deed by a woman adorned with godliness?

Scriptural Insight: One vivid example of a Christian widow doing good deeds is that of Dorcas. Her story is found in Acts 9:36-41. As Jesus said about Mary in Mark 14:8, "She did what she could."

What application will you make to adorn yourself with godliness?

As a Christian woman, you should also devote yourself to all kinds of good deeds for the same reasons as you have learned in the study of 1 Timothy so far. It reflects your devotion to God and is pleasing to Him. It represents Him well and gives glory to Him. It reflects His heart of compassion for people. And, it draws unbelievers to the gospel. You can probably think of a few more reasons. Remember that good deeds are a natural extension of adorning yourself with godliness.

21. As you consider your answers to questions 17-20,

- Give 1 or 2 examples of what you have done for someone else and how they responded to your action.

- Give 1 or 2 examples of what others have done for you and the difference it made in your life.

- Ask the Lord Jesus to guide you into doing good deeds that will demonstrate what you believe to be true about Christ and bring glory to Him.

Respond to the Lord about what you learned today.

DAY FOUR STUDY

Read 1 Timothy 5:1-16. Ask the Lord Jesus to teach you through His Word.

We will focus on vv. 11-15 in this session.

Paul distinguished three kinds of widows in the church. First, there were those who had "children or grandchildren" (physical relatives) who could financially support them (1 Timothy 5:4) and should take care of them. The second kind were those over 60 years old and had no one to care for them (1 Timothy 5:3,5,9). The church should care for them because they have no other source of dependence. The third group is those who give themselves to the pursuit of "pleasure" rather than the pursuit of God (1 Timothy 5:6). They did not qualify for regular support from the church.

What does it mean?

> **Scriptural Insight:** The pledge Paul referred to (1 Timothy 5:12) was probably a formal commitment, taken on joining the list of widows, wherein the woman vowed to serve Christ entirely without thought of marriage. In this way, she would devote herself without distraction to the Lord (1 Corinthians 7:34-35). (*The Bible Knowledge Commentary*, pg. 743)

22. According to vv. 11-12, why should younger widows not be put on the list?

> **Focus on the Meaning:** There is nothing wrong with a single woman wanting to marry. Marriage is honorable in God's sight. In that culture, a woman of marriageable age was expected to marry. The pledge would become like a trap to someone who should not have been encouraged to take it just because she needed financial help. Breaking it might have caused the woman to carry undue guilt. The leaders needed to be wise and compassionate concerning the younger widows.

23. Remember that widows were women first. What were some of the behaviors of the younger widows in Ephesus (v. 13)?

> **Focus on the Meaning:** These younger women may have been going from "house to house" or even house church to house church teaching spiritual content that was false (as in 1 Timothy 1:3-4). Nothing in the text suggests that Paul thought women were more prone than men to gossip. Indeed, gossip is not a female weakness; it is a human one. Sticking our noses into others' business is not a female weakness; it is a human one. And teaching false doctrine is not a male weakness; it is a human one. (Dr. Sandra Glahn, *"Does Paul Really Think Women are Gossips and Busybodies?"* accessed at Bible.org)

24. Why would women who are no longer married (or have no children at home) be tempted to get into the habit of being idle and busybodies?

From the Greek: "To be idle" means to be free from labor or even lazy, shunning the work one ought to perform." As they have developed the habit of being idle, they have become gossips (literally, "uttering or doing silly things, babbling") and busybodies, (literally, "busy about trifles and neglectful of important matters"). The word translated "busybodies" was also used for those practicing magic (Acts 19:19). Ephesus was the center for magic in the Roman world. From 1 Timothy 1:3-4 ; 1 Timothy 4:1-3; and 2 Timothy 3:5-7, you get a glimpse of the influence of false teaching on some of the women in Ephesus. Consider how breaking the pledge to not marry would have added to their guilt, making them vulnerable to false teaching.

25. In Ephesus, the younger women were not only developing the habit of being idle, they were also being disruptive by their foolish conversation (possibly even false teaching) and neglecting that which was important (1 Timothy 5:10). In what ways can an idle and disruptive person affect…?

- Herself—

- Others around her (family, neighbors, co-workers, an entire organization)—

26. Looking at vv. 14-15: What counsel did Paul give to the younger women (without mates or children) and why?

Think About It: In Paul's culture, the options he gave to the younger widows were the common experience for them. The household was the workplace for a typical woman with a family. In today's culture, particularly in the western world, unmarried women have many more options available to them in order to support themselves. Single moms, however, often still struggle financially, even those who are actively employed.

27. ***Deeper Discoveries (optional):*** Idleness was not related to just women in the Roman world. In Thessalonica, idleness was a common problem for both men and women (1 Thessalonians 5:14; 2 Thessalonians 3:6). Read 2 Thessalonians 3:12. To those who were being idle and disruptive busybodies in Thessalonica, what was Paul's counsel? In what ways was that similar to the counsel he gave in 1 Timothy 5:14?

What application will you make to adorn yourself with godliness?

28. Are opportunities to do good deeds limited to any particular age group or marital status of women? Are opportunities to be idle busybodies limited to any particular age group or marital status of women? Explain your answer.

29. Is there an idle and disruptive person affecting your life? Or, are you that idle and disruptive person affecting your life? How will you apply what you learned in this lesson if you are that one?

30. In Lesson Six, we saw several evidences of godliness displayed—devotion to God expressed in a life pleasing to Him. Feel free to add to the list in the chart below. Choose one example of godliness from this passage. Ask the Lord Jesus to give you a desire for that in your life and to adorn you with that. He has the power to make it happen.

Verse(s)	What godliness looks like
v. 4	*Caring for older widows in your family*
v. 5	*Putting your hope in God, asking Him for help as you need it*
v. 10	*Devoting yourself to good deeds that enhance and serve the family of God*
v. 12	*Not being idle busybodies who talk nonsense and teach error*

v. 14	*Managing your household well*

Respond to the Lord about what you learned today.

Recommended: Listen to the podcast "Godly Women Are Known by What They Do" after doing this lesson to reinforce what you have learned. Use the following listener guide.

Godly Women Are Known by What They Do

Luke chapter 8 tells us about a group of women who followed Jesus, traveling with Him and supporting the whole group of twelve disciples and their master out of their own resources. Their devotion to Him was expressed in a life that reflected Him and was pleasing to Him. What they started continued through the establishment of the New Testament church.

#1: GODLY WOMEN STAY USEFUL TO GOD AS THEY GROW OLD.

- Putting our hope in God, having Christ-like behavior, sharing Christ with nonbelievers, and doing good deeds for others has no retirement age.

- The righteous still bear fruit in old age, staying fresh and green. To stay fresh and green means to stay faithful to the Lord and useful to Him in bearing fruit. It is the opposite of developing hardened hearts. *Psalm 92:12-15*

- Older women adorned with godliness stay tuned to the needs of the women around them—all ages, young to old—and desire to reach them and teach them. They approach their Bible study with fresh eyes every day, looking for new things the Lord will be teaching them and thinking how they can share that with someone who needs to know it. Older women adorned with godliness stay aware of God's presence and work in their lives giving them a new song to share with others, not just what He did years ago.

- Staying fresh and green is a heart attitude and a choice we must make even through declining physical and mental capabilities. Older women can still adorn themselves with godliness just as much as any younger person can.

#2: GODLY WOMEN TAKE CARE OF THEIR OWN.

- A godly woman takes care of those within her own household or sphere of responsibility. *1 Timothy 5:4, 16.*

- Women who lived back then were women like we are today in many every day aspects of life. They had many of the same duties. And, they also had the same weaknesses that we have as women, including betrayal, direct verbal assault, jealousy, and backbiting.

- A woman adorning herself with godliness will put off those things that cause friction in the household or family and show kindness and forgiveness instead. When you are able to do this, then you are free to love those in your household who may not be easily lovable. You choose to love and care for those in your family, extended family, or other because of your devotion to God. *Ephesians 4:32*

#3: GODLY WOMEN INFLUENCE CHILDREN FOR CHRIST.

- The first example of a good deed listed in 1 Timothy 5:10 is "bringing up children." The Holy Spirit spoke through Paul to include this.

- Bringing up children can refer to children belonging to you or the children of others.

- A godly woman takes the opportunity presented to them to have an influence on children to trust in Jesus Christ and follow Him with their lives.

#4: GODLY WOMEN USE THEIR SOCIAL SKILLS TO BENEFIT THE BODY OF CHRIST.

- God created women to be social. Women are pretty good at building relationships with other women. After all, we have to share those 20,000 words per day with someone!

- Since God gave us this gift, He has the right to use it for His purposes. From 1 Timothy 5, we see that one of His purposes is to care for His people.

- God uses our social skills to care for His people by showing hospitality. Hospitality is opening up your home to share it with others.

- God also uses our social skills in serving one another in the local church. Washing the saints' feet just because a figure of speech for humble service in the church family.

- God uses our social skills to help others in trouble. Usually, it is through women that needs in the body get known to the church staff. And, women are the ones who jump right in and meet the need.

CONCLUSION

From 1 Timothy chapter 5, we can walk away with four applications for sure as we adorn ourselves with godliness.

- ✓ Godly women stay useful to God as they grow old. They don't retire from His service nor should they let themselves grow hardened and self-centered.

- ✓ Godly women take care of their own. They do what they can to resolve relationship conflicts with other women in their families and love on them even when those other women are hard to love.

- ✓ Godly women influence children for Christ in whatever manner and in whatever settings they are able to do so.

- ✓ And, godly women use their social skills to benefit the Body of Christ, serving others with humility and respect and taking care of needs that arise whenever possible.

"She has done a beautiful thing to me. ... She did what she could." (Mark 14:6,8)

That applies to all Christian women. From a heart that is devoted to our Lord Jesus Christ, we should do what we can for Him. How we live out our love for Him will be a beautiful thing to Him.

Being a woman of God is a dynamite position to have in life.

Let Jesus satisfy your heart with such love for God that you will want to live a life that pleases Him.

7: Reputation and Resources

1 Timothy 5:17-6:10

Day One Study—Get the Big Picture

Ask the Lord Jesus to teach you through His Word.

What does the Bible say?

Read the Bible passage below (NIV). Use your own method (colored pencils, lines, shapes) to mark 1) anything that grabs your attention, 2) words you want to understand, and 3) topics you have seen before in this letter. Draw arrows between thoughts that connect. Put a star ✱ next to anything you think relates to godliness.

5 *17 The elders who direct the affairs of the church well are worthy of double honor, especially those whose work is preaching and teaching. 18 For Scripture says, "Do not muzzle an ox while it is treading out the grain," and "The worker deserves his wages." 19 Do not entertain an accusation against an elder unless it is brought by two or three witnesses. 20 But those elders who are sinning you are to reprove before everyone, so that the others may take warning. 21 I charge you, in the sight of God and Christ Jesus and the elect angels, to keep these instructions without partiality, and to do nothing out of favoritism.*

22 Do not be hasty in the laying on of hands, and do not share in the sins of others. Keep yourself pure.

23 Stop drinking only water, and use a little wine because of your stomach and your frequent illnesses.

24 The sins of some are obvious, reaching the place of judgment ahead of them; the sins of others trail behind them. 25 In the same way, good deeds are obvious, and even those that are not obvious cannot remain hidden forever.

6 *1 All who are under the yoke of slavery should consider their masters worthy of full respect, so that God's name and our teaching may not be slandered. 2 Those who have believing masters should not show them disrespect just because they are fellow believers. Instead, they should serve them even better because their masters are dear to them as fellow believers and are devoted to the welfare of their slaves.*

These are the things you are to teach and insist on. 3 If anyone teaches otherwise and does not agree to the sound instruction of our Lord Jesus Christ and to godly teaching, 4 they are conceited and understand nothing. They have an unhealthy interest in controversies and quarrels about words that result in envy, strife, malicious talk, evil suspicions 5 and constant friction between people of corrupt mind, who have been robbed of the truth and who think that godliness is a means to financial gain.

6 But godliness with contentment is great gain. 7 For we brought nothing into the world, and we can take nothing out of it. 8 But if we have food and clothing, we will be content with that. 9 Those who want to get rich fall into temptation and a trap and into many foolish and harmful desires that plunge people into ruin and destruction. 10 For the love of money is a root of all kinds of evil. Some people, eager for money, have wandered from the faith and pierced themselves with many griefs.

1. What grabbed your attention from 1 Timothy 5:17-6:10?

2. What verses or specific words do you want to understand better?

3. What words or phrases are repeated in this passage? Give verses.

4. What topics (if any) in this passage have we studied in previous lessons? Give verses.

5. What verses illustrate or help you understand what godliness looks like?

6. ***Adorn yourself with godliness:*** From this lesson's passage (1 Timothy 5:17-6:10), choose one verse to dwell upon all week long. Write it in the space below. Ask God to teach you through this verse.

Respond to the Lord about what you learned today.

DAY TWO STUDY

Read 1 Timothy 5:17-25. Ask the Lord Jesus to teach you through His Word.

We will focus on vv. 17-22 in this session.

What does it mean?

Another group (besides the widows) deserved Timothy's special attention: elders. This is not referring to any older men in the congregation but those who are designated to fill the office of elder. We covered the qualifications for church elders in Lesson 4 (1 Timothy 3:1-7).

7. **Deeper Discoveries (optional):** Read 1 Timothy 5:17; Titus 1:9; Acts 20:28-31; and 1 Peter 5:1-3 to answer the question, "What are the responsibilities of the elders to the local church?"

8. Focusing on 1 Timothy 5:17-20:

   • What is the local church's responsibility toward elders who rule well (vv. 17, 19)?

   Scriptural Insight: The Greek word for "honor" is the same word used in 1 Timothy 5:3 where it refers to respect (proper recognition). Verse 17 allows for a division of labor among the elders, though all were to be "able to teach" (1 Timothy 3:2). (*Dr. Constable's Notes on 1 Timothy 2020 Edition,* pp. 109-110)

   • Paul's words in v. 18 give reasons for financially supporting those whose work in the church was preaching and teaching. What reasons did he give?

   Scriptural Insight: The first quote is from Deuteronomy 25:4. The second quote is from Luke 10:7. Either he was quoting from the book of Luke already written, or he was quoting what he knew to be something that Jesus said.

   • Read Luke 10:1-7 for Jesus' instructions to His disciples who were being sent out to minister to people.

9. Criticism of leaders is a common experience in churches.

   • What were Paul's instructions on how a church should handle accusations against an elder?

   • What are Jesus' instructions in Matthew 18:15-17 for dealing with recognized sin in the church?

   • What could happen when this isn't handled correctly, and how would this affect a church?

10. Focusing on vv. 21-22.

   • What advice did Paul give to Timothy? Note: Laying on of hands refers to the ordaining of someone for an official position.

   • How did that advice fit with the instructions about elders given in vv. 17-20?

   • Besides the church members, who are also the witnesses to everything happening in a local church (v. 21)? See also 1 Peter 1:12.

      Focus on the Meaning: Who were the "elect" angels? These are the ones who have chosen to stay faithful to God and not rebel against Him like Satan and the demons. The word elect means "chosen and appointed." Even the Messiah is called "elect" because He had an appointed position and purpose.

   • How should remembering those witnesses affect how we abide by biblical instruction?

Scriptural Insight: Paul often reminds his readers that God the Father and Jesus Christ are both witnesses to everything that he says and does. See 1 Timothy 6:13; 2 Timothy 2:14 and 4:1.

What application will you make to adorn yourself with godliness?

11. Criticism of leaders (1 Timothy 5:19) is a temptation for both men and women in a church. The general principle laid out by Jesus Christ is to go to the person first and check out the information that you have heard or experienced (Matthew 18:15-17). If that doesn't solve the issue, go directly to the one in authority over that person. Do not talk about it with others in general conversation like the younger widows were doing in Ephesus (1 Timothy 5:13). I call that "sharing sensitive information (personal and/or confidential) in inappropriate settings (with those who don't need to know that information)." Use discretion when dealing with ministry concerns by only talking with those directly responsible for the solution.

- Do you have a tendency to talk about the faults of your leaders or a ministry in general conversation, thus spreading discontent beyond yourself?

- Based upon what you learned in this lesson, what will you do next time you see or hear about a ministry leader in your church doing something wrong or have a disagreement with a ministry leader?

12. Favoritism or partiality (1 Timothy 5:21) is often denounced in Scripture (Leviticus 19:15; James 2:1-13). The problem with favoritism or partiality is that it blinds you to the faults of others. Recognizing certain people to be leaders of a ministry because of their qualifications is not favoritism (1 Timothy 3:1-13). Giving preference or showing partiality to someone because they are rich, famous, or have status is favoritism.

As a ministry leader:

- Why should you avoid favoritism or partiality when asking women to be ministry leaders, even of a small group? Consider what you have learned so far in 1 Timothy.

- What steps do you take to avoid favoritism or partiality when asking women to be ministry leaders, even of a small group?

As a church member:

- What steps do you / should you take to avoid favoritism or partiality in your relationships within the local church body?

Respond to the Lord about what you learned today.

DAY THREE STUDY

Read 1 Timothy 5:17-6:2. Ask the Lord Jesus to teach you through His Word.

We will focus on 5:23-6:2 in this session.

What does it mean?

> **Focus on the Meaning:** Verse 23 is a side note from Paul to Timothy. Paul may have realized that the process of elder discipline, that he imposed on Timothy, would have been hard on him physically as well as emotionally. According to this verse, Timothy suffered from frequent illness. Consequently, the apostle prescribed a little wine for medicinal purposes. Wine was one of the chief remedial agents of those times in which the science of medicine was in its infancy among Greek physicians. (*Dr. Constable's Notes on 1 Timothy 2020 Edition*, p. 113)

13. Focus on vv. 24-25:

   - What did Paul say about a person's sins?

   - What could "trail behind them" mean? See Proverbs 10:9 and any other verses that apply.

   - What did Paul say about a person's good deeds? Why is that?

Focusing on 1 Timothy 6:1-2:

Continuing what he had being doing throughout 1 Timothy 5, Paul urged the adoption of godly attitudes and behavior toward others in specific roles or circumstances. Slavery, like widowhood, was a common experience for many of the Christians. Typical households of the time included both slaves and hired servants. Nearly 1 out of every 2 men, women, and children in the Roman Empire were slaves. Slavery was economic rather than racially motivated. People usually became slaves as a result of war (taken captive) or poverty (indentured to pay off a debt). The Bible doesn't condone the practice of slavery. God declared in Jeremiah 34:14-15 that freeing indentured slaves was right in His sight. Wherever the gospel has taken hold, the institution of slavery has been abolished in most of the world. Sadly, slavery in some form still exists.

> **Scriptural Insight:** A great social and legal gulf separated masters and slaves or hired servants. But when a master and his slave became Christians, they became spiritual equals, brothers (and sisters) in Christ Jesus (Galatians 3:28). Equality in the church but inviolable separation at home obviously made for interesting interpersonal relations in and out of the church. (*Life Application Bible Study Guide*, pg. 114)

Paul gave counsel about master / slave relationships in 6 of his letters (1 Corinthians, Ephesians, Colossians, 1 Timothy, Titus, and Philemon). All Christian slaves or masters—whether older, younger, male, or female—were to adorn themselves with godliness as individuals. The counsel for the master / slave relationship was in the context of a work place. Households were work places. Slaves worked for masters. Masters managed and determined work tasks for workers in their households—both slave and free.

We can look at these verses and, like elsewhere in Scripture, draw principles of godly behavior that can apply to any similar situation. Everyone today works in some fashion so the principles can apply. First, we'll look at what the text says, then we'll apply the principles to the modern workplace (which includes the household).

14. Read the following verses to answer the question, "What counsel did Paul give to those under the "yoke of slavery" and why?

- 1 Timothy 6:1-2—

- Ephesians 6:5-8—

- Colossians 3:22-25—

- 1 Corinthians 7:21-22—

> **Dependent Living:** "If you can gain your freedom (1 Corinthians 7:21-22)" can apply to any work situation in which you find yourself. What if you hate what you do for work? If the work is immoral, definitely get out of it. If the work itself is beneficial, but you don't like it, that's where you submit yourself to Jesus Christ as Lord over you and even over that job. Let Him teach you how to be thankful for that work or lead you to something else. Whatever He brings into your life that makes you more dependent upon Him is good for you. Work is a great environment to learn that.

15. From Ephesians 6:9 and Colossians 4:1, what counsel did Paul give to "slave masters" who were also Christians and why?

Historical Insight: Paul's modification of the servant-master relationship in [Colossians 3:22-25] and Ephesians 6:5-9 destroyed the very essence of slavery. Also, the New Testament consistently calls Christians to a role as servants (Mark 10:43-45)." While not condoning slavery or calling for its dissolution, Paul makes it clear that the deeper and more significant relationship is that between two believers rather than how society defines their relationship on the surface. (*Dr. Constable's Notes on 1 Timothy 2020 Edition,* p. 116)

16. ***Deeper Discoveries (optional):*** Read Paul's letter to Philemon (a Christian slave master) about his slave (Onesimus) who had stolen money and run away but was now a Christian and wanted to return home. What counsel did Paul give regarding this situation?

Now, let's apply the principles of godliness that you saw in the passages you just studied to the modern workplace. Consider "master" to be an employer or a manager. Consider "slave" to be an employee.

17. What principles of godly behavior can be applied from an employer's or manager's perspective?

Think About It: If more Christian employees today served their employers with genuine concern and as though they were serving God, quality and productivity would increase dramatically...If employers...today manifested this kind of compassionate and impartial care for their employees, certainly their employees' motivation to work would radically improve. (*The Bible Knowledge Commentary New Testament,* p. 683)

18. What principles of godly behavior can be applied from an employee's perspective?

> **Think About It:** This view of work transforms a worker's attitudes and performance. Even the most servile work thereby becomes a ministry and an act of worship. All jobs can and should be "full-time Christian work." (*Dr. Constable's Notes on Colossians 2020 Edition*, p. 88)

What application will you make to adorn yourself with godliness?

19. *Your work:* When you are working in an office or on the factory floor or in your home, you are serving Jesus Christ with your work. Your everyday run of the mill job can be as much a sacred ministry for the Lord as teaching Sunday School. Your work is an act of worship, not a curse. Your workplace (be it home, office, factory floor, school room, or road construction) is your mission field. Your work environment is where you must intentionally practice letting Jesus live His life through you—in difficult situations, with challenging people, and with integrity that honors the Lord Jesus Christ. It is where you adorn yourself with godliness.

- Do you view your work in this way? Why or why not?

- How can you specifically apply what you learned in this lesson to adorn yourself with godliness in your current work setting, including volunteer work?

- Ask the Lord Jesus to give you the mindset and heart that everything you do in any work setting is for Him first then for others. Ask Him to adorn you with godliness in your work environment so that God's name may not be slandered (1 Timothy 6:1). It's okay to say, *"Lord Jesus, I can't do this on my own. I trust you to do this in me and through me."* Then, watch what He does!

Respond to the Lord about what you learned today.

DAY FOUR STUDY

Read 1 Timothy 5:17-6:10. Ask the Lord Jesus to teach you through His Word.

We will focus on 6:3-10 in this session.

What does it mean?

In vv. 2-3, Paul once again reinforced the necessity of teaching and insisting on truth and sound doctrine. See 1 Timothy 4:6, 11 and 5:7, 21. Then, he returned to his initial warnings about false teachers (vv. 4-5).

20. Review 1 Timothy 1:3-4, 6-7 and 4:1-3 to see what the false teachers were teaching.

- According to 1 Timothy 6:4-5, what words did Paul use to describe anyone who does not agree to the sound "instruction of our Lord Jesus Christ and to godly teaching" (v. 3)?

- Their unhealthy interest in controversies and quarrels about words" (vv. 4-5) caused what in the church?

Focus on the Meaning: In these verses, Paul issued a kind of "wanted poster." It is the opposite of the job descriptions of godly men given in chapter 3. The false teachers in Ephesus advocated "doctrine" that was "different" from what Scripture and the apostles taught. They disagreed with the teachings of the "Lord Jesus Christ," that fostered spiritual health in those who heard and responded to them. Furthermore, they rejected the doctrine that conforms to, and results in, godly behavior ("godliness"). (*Dr. Constable's Notes on 1 Timothy 2020 Edition*, pp. 116-117)

21. When these behaviors are occurring in the church,

- How might they affect the people in the church? See also 1 Timothy 1:4.

- How might they affect an outsider's view of the church?

22. At the end of v. 5, we see a motivation for the false teachers and those who follow them.

- What is it?

- What could that mean?

Scriptural Insight: The pagan world of Ephesus believed that the way to be content was to be really wealthy. Notice the irony in 1 Timothy 6:5 as Paul points out that those men who think that godliness is a means to financial gain are actually "robbed" or "deprived" of the truth themselves. The atmosphere surrounding those same men is described as one of "constant friction" (v 5).

Focusing on vv. 6-10:

23. The error stated in 1 Timothy 6:5 is that godliness is a means to financial gain. This false teaching is still prevalent in our world today, often taught as the "prosperity gospel." Several verses in today's passage are often quoted, so let's pay attention to the context around the familiar verses.

    • What does Paul say is truly "great gain" (v. 6)?

    • Define contentment.

    We have seen many illustrations of godliness in this letter. We can know what it looks like. An attitude of contentment regarding one's material possessions is one more way we can adorn ourselves with godliness. Notice the humbling truths found in vv. 7-8. "Food and clothing" were synonymous with the basic necessities of life.

    • Read Philippians 4:11-13. What do you learn about the issue of contentment from Paul's example?

24. ***Deeper Discoveries (optional):*** Read Matthew 6:24-34 and Luke 12:16-32. What truths should be the foundation of being content with basic material possessions?

25. According to 1 Timothy 6:9-10,

    • What are the dangers to those whose goal in life is to get rich (v. 9)?

    • How have you seen this to be true in life today?

Scriptural Insight: There are approximately 500 verses on prayer (in the Bible), fewer than 500 on faith, but more that 2,350 verses on how to handle money. Moreover, Jesus Christ said more about money than any other subject. (*Crown Ministries Small Group Financial Study,* pg. 9)

26. The Bible says in 1 Timothy 6:10, "The love of money is a root of all kinds of evil." It is not the money itself. Money is simply a tool we can use to bring glory to God. The problem is the love of it becomes a root (not the only root) of all kinds of evil (v. 9).

    - In what ways can the "love of money" be a **root** of all kinds of evil? Consider all possibilities, including what Paul mentioned in the second part of v. 10.

    - Of the 2 results in v. 10, which is the worst and why?

    Think About It: Materialism is a desire to possess things instead of a love for the God who made those things. That shows up here in this verse. It is possible to have very little money and yet to love it. Some people have much money yet do not love it. Love of money contrasts with love of God and neighbor, the two greatest commandments (Matt. 22:39; cf. Matt. 6:24; Luke 16:13; 1 John 2:15). (*Dr. Constable's Notes on 1 Timothy 2020 Edition,* pp. 119, 121)

27. Considering what you have learned in this passage, why can godliness with contentment be great gain?

28. ***Deeper Discoveries (optional):*** Read the following verses in which the Bible addresses the relationships of money and our hearts. Take time to think carefully about each verse then write a summary of what you've learned. 1 Chronicles 29:11,12; Matthew 6:19-21, 24; 2 Corinthians 9:6-11; and any other verses you can find.

What application will you make to adorn yourself with godliness?

29. *Regarding contentment about material possessions:* Do you find yourself resentful of others and what they have (material possessions), or discouraged by what you don't have? Do you want to be content?

   - Ask the Lord Jesus to reveal any "love for money" in your heart and mind. Then, ask Him to replace that with a greater love for Him than anything that money could ever provide for you. This will lead you to being a God-dependent woman more than a money-dependent woman.

   - Focus on what He has already provided for you. Make a list of a few things God has richly given you to enjoy and thank Him for it.

   - Make the decision to not fret over what you do not have and to refuse to covet what others may have. List a few of those things here and give them to Him.

   - Money is a tool we can use for God's glory. What do you most want to accomplish with the money God has entrusted to you as you live out your life on earth?

   Think About It: If you are afraid that perhaps the love of money is getting a hold on your soul, start giving some of it away and see how you feel! If you feel really glad then you are still safe, but if it almost breaks your heart then it is time to get down on your knees and pray to be freed from this sin of covetousness! It is going to ruin you unless you are delivered from it. (*Dr. Constable's Notes on 1 Timothy 2020 Edition*, p. 123)

30. In Lesson Seven, we saw several evidences of godliness displayed—devotion to God expressed in a life pleasing to Him. Feel free to add to the list in the chart below. Choose one example of godliness from this passage. Ask the Lord Jesus to give you a desire for that in your life and to adorn you with that. He has the power to make it happen.

Verse(s)	What godliness looks like
6:1-2	*Do your work in such a way that honors God's name*
6:1-2	*Be the best employee or employer that you can be for the sake of Christ.*

6:3-4	Recognize and avoid teachers who are conceited and rebel against the sound instruction of Christ
6:8	Be content with the basic provisions that God provides you
6:10	Love God more than money

Respond to the Lord about what you learned today.

Recommended: Listen to the podcast "Godliness Views Work as More than a Paycheck" after doing this lesson to reinforce what you have learned. Use the following listener guide.

Godliness Views Work as More than a Paycheck

Work in any culture is…well, work. Sometimes enjoyable. Often hard and exhausting. Sometimes challenging because of the people with whom you work rather than the work itself. When you're working with your God-given skills, all work can be an expression of your devotion to God. And, adorning yourself with godliness applies to your work.

MORE THAN A PAYCHECK

> *"Whatever you do, work at it with all your heart, as **working for the Lord**, not for human masters, since you know that you will receive an inheritance from the Lord as a reward. It **is the Lord Christ you are serving.**" (Colossians 3:23-24)*

- Your workplace, wherever that may be, is your mission field. Your work environment is where you must intentionally practice letting Jesus live His life through you—in difficult situations, with challenging people, and with integrity that honors the Lord Jesus Christ.

A FEW TRUTHS ABOUT ANY KIND OF WORK

It always helps to know a few truths about work—any kind of work.

- **Truth #1: Work is God's idea.** God is a worker. God created work in the beginning before sin ever entered into His world. Work is good. Sin corrupted work so it got a lot harder to do. Then, Jesus came along to renew us and restore our approach to work as He lives in us and through us. We are free to work for God's glory now.

- **Truth #2: Work is an avenue for accomplishing God's mission.** When Jesus commissioned all of His followers to make disciples everywhere they went, none of them were on church staff or in mission organizations. They were ordinary people going to work every day. In the same way, we are Jesus' ambassadors at work—in the conference room, on the hospital floor, at the lunch break, in the classroom, and in the kitchen. As we do our work with integrity and intentionally build relationships with our coworkers, clients or family members, Jesus is actively involved in that. Work is your mission field and your platform to let Christ live His life through you.

- **Truth #3: Work is the place where God grows us into maturity.** The Spirit of God uses our relationships, successes, failures, and experiences at work as tools in our spiritual growth. He teaches us to have the mind of Christ at work, to treat people as Jesus did, and to grow in our jobs under His guidance. God uses our work to mature us.

- **Truth #4: Work has purpose beyond ourselves.** God can do more with our work than we can imagine. God designed work for the good of the world—not just for ourselves. Our work impacts the people in our work environment, our clients, and our managers. Work provides jobs, fuels the economy, and allows culture to flourish. When we work, we can taste the goodness of God intended for work in the beginning.

- **Truth #5: Work is where we practice godliness.** All those exhortations in 1 Timothy 4:12—setting an example in speech, in conduct, in love, in faith, and in purity—all those apply at work. In Colossians 3:17, we are reminded to do everything we say or do in light of Jesus as Lord. Jesus is Lord over our work. Employees or managers, Jesus is Lord over your work. Business owners, Jesus is Lord over your business. So, your work represents your devotion to Him. It is worship. And, we glorify Him as we do our jobs well.

- **Truth #6: Work can become an addiction that takes the focus off of Christ and puts it on yourself instead.** You know that you have let work become an addiction when you are obsessively thinking about freeing up more time for your work. When you develop health problems because of work-related stress and over-work, that's not working for the Lord. Another clue is when you use your work to maintain your self-worth. The modern term for that is workism. Workism is the belief that your work is the center of your identity. For a Christian, your work should never be the center of your identity. Christ is. So, if you recognize this in yourself, go to the Lord and ask Him to free you from the addiction. Talk to a counsellor about this as well.

- What if you are retired from income-producing work? How is your attitude toward the work that you did? Are you bad-mouthing it? Or, can you now look back with gratitude that you had that opportunity to worship God with your work?

A FEW QUESTIONS ABOUT FAITH IN THE WORKPLACE

- *How do you live out your faith in your workplace?* As I mentioned before, you do that by adorning yourself with the godly behavior you've seen taught in 1 Timothy. That's recognizing Jesus Christ as Lord of your life and Lord of your behavior. Let Him live His life through you to invite others around you to want to know Him. Ask Jesus to help you do that and trust Him to work in you and through you.

- *What is legal to do at work?* Go to firstliberty.org to find out what is legal for a Christian to do in any workplace. That's firstliberty.org. You might be surprised by what you can legally do to live out your faith in the marketplace. And be grateful for that.

- *How do you invest in your co-workers without stealing time from your employer?* You use whatever break time or interaction opportunities you have available to get to know your co-workers and minister to them. Ask Jesus to help you be creative and caring. I have several Bible Studies you could offer that are short and easy and would fit nicely in a lunch hour time frame.

- *What if you hate what you do for work?* That's where you submit yourself to Jesus Christ as Lord over you and even over that job. Let Him teach you how to be thankful for that work or lead you to something else. Whatever He brings into your life that makes you more dependent upon Him is good for you. Work is a great environment to learn that.

Remember this. Your work belongs to Jesus. He will enable you to find purpose in it that brings glory to Him. So, keep working diligently, producing what is needed, providing for yourself and others, and preparing the way for others to see Christ in you. Godliness views work as more than a paycheck. It has a greater purpose. Are you onboard with that?

Let Jesus satisfy your heart with such love for God that you will want to live a life that pleases Him.

8: Pursue Godliness

1 Timothy 6:11-21

DAY ONE STUDY—GET THE BIG PICTURE

Ask the Lord Jesus to teach you through His Word.

What does the Bible say?

Read the Bible passage below (NIV) including verses from the last lesson. Use your own method (colored pencils, lines, shapes) to mark 1) anything that grabs your attention, 2) words you want to understand, and 3) topics you have seen before in this letter. Draw arrows between thoughts that connect. Put a star ✱ next to anything you think relates to godliness.

6 *⁶ But godliness with contentment is great gain. ⁷ For we brought nothing into the world, and we can take nothing out of it. ⁸ But if we have food and clothing, we will be content with that. ⁹ Those who want to get rich fall into temptation and a trap and into many foolish and harmful desires that plunge people into ruin and destruction. ¹⁰ For the love of money is a root of all kinds of evil. Some people, eager for money, have wandered from the faith and pierced themselves with many griefs.*

¹¹ But you, man of God, flee from all this, and pursue righteousness, godliness, faith, love, endurance and gentleness. ¹² Fight the good fight of the faith. Take hold of the eternal life to which you were called when you made your good confession in the presence of many witnesses. ¹³ In the sight of God, who gives life to everything, and of Christ Jesus, who while testifying before Pontius Pilate made the good confession, I charge you ¹⁴ to keep this command without spot or blame until the appearing of our Lord Jesus Christ, ¹⁵ which God will bring about in his own time—God, the blessed and only Ruler, the King of kings and Lord of lords, ¹⁶ who alone is immortal and who lives in unapproachable light, whom no one has seen or can see. To him be honor and might forever. Amen.

¹⁷ Command those who are rich in this present world not to be arrogant nor to put their hope in wealth, which is so uncertain, but to put their hope in God, who richly provides us with everything for our enjoyment. ¹⁸ Command them to do good, to be rich in good deeds, and to be generous and willing to share. ¹⁹ In this way they will lay up treasure for themselves as a firm foundation for the coming age, so that they may take hold of the life that is truly life.

²⁰ Timothy, guard what has been entrusted to your care. Turn away from godless chatter and the opposing ideas of what is falsely called knowledge, ²¹ which some have professed and in so doing have departed from the faith.

Grace be with you all.

1. What grabbed your attention from 1 Timothy 6:11-21?

2. What verses or specific words do you want to understand better?

3. What words or phrases are repeated in this passage? Give verses.

4. What topics (if any) in this passage have we studied in previous lessons? Give verses.

5. What verses illustrate or help you understand what godliness looks like?

6. ***Adorn yourself with godliness:*** From this lesson's passage (1 Timothy 6:11-21), choose one verse to dwell upon all week long. Write it in the space below. Ask God to teach you through this verse.

Respond to the Lord about what you learned today.

Day Two Study

Read 1 Timothy 6:11-21. Ask the Lord Jesus to teach you through His Word.

We will focus on vv. 11-16 in this session.

What does it mean?

7. Verse 11 begins with the phrase, "But you, man of God, flee from these things…." This applies not only to those in a position of church authority but also to every believer. The truth is that you are God's. You are a man of God or a woman of God. As someone belonging to God, from what are you to flee (vv. 9-10)?

8. As you choose to flee from the ungodliness that can trap you and ruin you,

   • What are you to pursue instead (v. 11)?

   • Why would you pursue these instead? Remember you are a woman of God, devoted to Him (v. 11).

   Focus on the Meaning: "Righteousness" includes all attitudes and actions in harmony with what God calls right. "Godliness" is devotion to God that is expressed in godlike character and conduct. "Faith" is trust in God. "Love" is selfless devotion to the needs of others. "Endurance" is faithful continuance through adverse or discouraging circumstances. "Gentleness" is tender kindness toward others. (*Dr. Constable's Notes on 1 Timothy 2020 Edition,* p. 124)

9. While you are pursuing godliness and those other godly virtues in v. 11,

   • What must you also do (v. 12)?

   • This is a spiritual battle, not a physical one. As such, who / what are you fighting against? Consider what you've learned in 1 Timothy. See also Ephesians 6:12; 2 Corinthians 10:3-4; and other verses that apply.

- With what weapons do you fight the good fight of faith? See also Hebrews 4:12 and other verses that apply.

Focus on the Meaning: "Take hold of the eternal life to which you were called." Eternal life begins the moment you are saved. Your hope is your future in heaven, but you can live abundantly now as a Spirit-indwelt woman of God. Live that victorious, abundant life now!

10. Looking at the charge Paul made to Timothy in vv. 13-14, Paul made similar appeals to Timothy throughout this letter, sighting the witnesses.

- What had Paul said in 1 Timothy 5:21?

- What is the "charge" here in 1 Timothy 6:13-14? Note: This command refers to the entire body of sound teaching Paul had been describing throughout the letter.

- Why is it important for Timothy, and you, to be without spot or blame? Whose reputation is at stake? See 1 Timothy 3:7 and 6:1.

11. Look at all the descriptions of the attributes of God given in vv. 13-16. Make a list of everything you learn about God from those verses. Compare to what you read in 1 Timothy 1:17.

Historical Insight: Ephesus was not only the haven of Artemis, but an early center of emperor worship as well. This doxology, therefore, is Paul's parting shot that the God with whom the church has to do in the gospel of Christ is none other than the supreme Ruler of the universe, the Lord over all other lords. (*Dr. Constable's Notes on 1 Timothy 2020 Edition*, pp. 127-128)

12. ***Deeper Discoveries (optional):*** The appearing of the Lord Jesus Christ is ever present in Paul's letters. It is a promise to all believers that Jesus will come back to gather His own and then set up His kingdom on earth. Only God knows and determines when this will be. Read 1 Thessalonians 1:10; 3:13; 4:13-17; 5:23; Philippians 3:20-21; and Titus 2:13-14. He is our blessed hope. Why? What hope do we have in His appearing again?

What application will you make to adorn yourself with godliness?

13. In what ways have you or do you "fight the good fight of faith" in your life?

> **Think About It:** One way to fight the good fight of faith is to pray for an unbeliever in your life to know Christ. Consider one person for whom you can specifically pray for their salvation throughout the remainder of this study. If you are in a group, each person should share with the whole group the name and relationship of that person.

14. ***Respond to the Lord about what you learned about Him.*** As seen in 1 Timothy 6:13-16 and 1:17, our God reveals Himself to us so that we can know Him well. You have a God you can truly know—not just head knowledge, but also be intimately acquainted with Him in your heart. Read Ephesians 1:17-23. Ask the Lord through His Spirit to open the eyes of your heart so you can know Him well and know the hope of everything He has given you now and plans to give you in the future. Feel free to use any creative means to respond as an act of praise just as Paul did in 1 Timothy 1:17.

> **Think About It:** True godliness engages our affections and awakens within us a desire to enjoy God's presence and fellowship. It produces a longing for God Himself. (Jerry Bridges, *The Practice of Godliness*)

DAY THREE STUDY

Read 1 Timothy 6:11-21. Ask the Lord Jesus to teach you through His Word.

We will focus on vv. 17-19 in this session.

What does it mean?

After the beautiful time of praise to the God of all provision, Paul went back to money matters. Jesus Christ, who is our witness, lived a life without spot or blame even in the area of money. So, we can follow His example and do the same.

15. For those who are rich in this present world, what are they *not* to do (v. 17 first part) and why? See also Jeremiah 9:23-24.

> **Think About It:** Those who spend more than they make, trusting that future income will cover their present overspending, are trusting in uncertain riches. (*Dr. Constable's Notes on 1 Timothy 2020 Edition*, p. 128)

16. What are those who are rich in this present world to do instead (v. 17 second part) and why?

17. Putting your hope in God is for everyone, not just rich believers (1 Timothy 5:5). Why is putting our hope in God the only way to "richly" enjoy life?

18. While putting our hope in God, whether rich or not rich,

- What are we to do (v. 18)?

- Why (v. 19)?

Think About It: We are all to view our money as God's enablement to accomplish good deeds (being willing to share). Once again, godliness is displayed through good deeds that all can see.

19. Being generous and willing to share is not related to how much money you have. It is still related to putting your hope in God. Read 2 Corinthians 8:2-5.

- I've given you verse 2 from the NIV in the chart below. Write verse 2 from any three other Bible translations.

NIV	*In the midst of a very severe trial, their overflowing joy and their extreme poverty welled up in rich generosity.*

- What is so amazing and radical about v. 2?

- Entirely on their own, what did they do (v. 4)?

- By what process did they do this (v. 5)?

Dependent Living: While undergoing severe trials, afflictions, and extreme poverty, overflowing joy yielded rich generosity. Paul never mentioned the size of their gift. What counts as "rich generosity?" R. G. LeTourneau, a rich businessman who created the first massive earth-moving machines, would often quote this little poem, *"It is not what you'd do with a million, if riches should ever be your lot. But what you are doing at present with the dollar and a quarter you've got."* So true! It's all about trusting God and relying on Him more than on yourself.

What application will you make to adorn yourself with godliness?

20. Look at what the Scripture says our attitude towards money and prosperity should be in vv. 17-19.

- What has God given you richly to enjoy?

- In what ways are you "generous and willing to share?"

- How will you apply what you learned in this lesson to your life today?

Respond to the Lord about what you learned today.

DAY FOUR STUDY

Read 1 Timothy 6:11-21. Ask the Lord Jesus to teach you through His Word.

We will focus on vv. 20-21 and some review of 1 Timothy in this session.

What does it say?

21. Paul closed with a final reminder of things he had already mentioned several times in his letter (vv. 20-21). What is the reminder?

What does it mean?

22. To what was Paul referring when he said, "Guard what has been entrusted to your care?" Look back through 1 Timothy. See also 2 Timothy 1:14.

23. To what was Paul referring when he said, "Turn away from godless chatter and the opposing ideas of what is falsely called knowledge?" Look back through 1 Timothy. See also 2 Timothy 2:14-18.

From the Greek: What did Paul mean by "falsely called knowledge?" The Greek word for knowledge is *gnosis*. Many scholars think this is a reference to the early stages of Gnostic influence. "Gnostics" taught that there was a higher knowledge, available only to the initiates of their cult. Paul had already set forth his full rebuttal to their contention in his letter to the Colossians (especially chapters 1 and 2). The false teaching in Ephesus was masquerading as spiritual knowledge. Instead of drawing people to Christ for their sufficiency, it drew them away from Christ.

24. Unlike most of his other letters, you will notice that there are no final greetings to individuals in the church there in Ephesus.

 • At the end of v. 21, what were Paul's words of reminder and hope to Timothy and the Ephesian church (you all, or in Texas, y'all)?

 • What does that mean to them and to us? Review the definition of grace in Lesson 2, Day 2.

What application will you make to adorn yourself with godliness?

25. *Falsely called knowledge:* We live in an educated society where scholarly people tell us they know better and are wiser than we are and that we should listen to them even when what they teach is against the plain truth of the Bible. Women should pursue education whenever possible.

 • Read 1 Corinthians 8:1. What can result from an emphasis on pursuing knowledge?

 • How does a Christian woman avoid that result and pursue godliness while she is acquiring knowledge through education?

- How do you determine if what you are reading or being taught is truth or manipulated to appear as truth?

26. What has been the most significant truth you learned through this study of 1 Timothy? Why?

Historical Insight: As mentioned earlier, Timothy was in Ephesus when Paul wrote 2 Timothy a couple of years later. Whether he ever made it to Rome before Paul's execution, we do not know. According to Foxe's Book of Martyrs, which was written several centuries later (originally published in 1563), Timothy remained in Ephesus until 97 A.D. During a pagan celebration of a feast called "Catagogian," Timothy severely reproved the people in the procession for their ridiculous idolatry. This antagonized the partygoers who beat him with clubs "in so dreadful a manner that he expired of the bruises two days later." We'll see him in heaven! The Ephesian church continued to play a prominent role in the history of the early church. A long line of bishops made Ephesus their headquarters. There is no longer a city of Ephesus, only an archeological site, and hardly any Christians to be found in the region. But, the wonderful teaching that the Ephesians received has been preserved for us by the Spirit in the book of Acts and 3 of Paul's letters—Ephesians, 1 Timothy and 2 Timothy.

27. In Lesson Eight, we saw several evidences of godliness displayed—devotion to God expressed in a life pleasing to Him. Feel free to add to the list in the chart below. Choose one example of godliness from this passage. Ask the Lord Jesus to give you a desire for that in your life and to adorn you with that. He has the power to make it happen.

Verse(s)	What godliness looks like
v. 11	Pursue righteousness, godliness, faith, love, endurance, and gentleness.
v. 12	Fight the good fight of the faith rather than giving it up to deception.
v. 14	Live your life in view of Christ's appearing at any time
vv. 15-16	Giving honor to God as your king and Lord
v. 17	Putting your hope in God rather than in money
v. 18	Being rich in good deeds, generous, and willing to share what God has provided you

Respond to the Lord about what you learned today.

Recommended: Listen to the podcast "Pursue Godliness Regarding Worldly Wealth" after doing this lesson to reinforce what you have learned. Use the following listener guide.

Pursue Godliness Regarding Worldly Wealth

Regarding God's provision and worldly wealth, Christians should think differently from the world. Give yourself to the Lord first. Pursue what matters to God—His honor and His purposes—more than your own. Pursue godliness even in matters of worldly wealth.

LESSON #1: GOD'S PROVISION IS HIS TO GIVE AND TAKE AWAY. REGARD IT HUMBLY.

We need to understand several facts about this lesson.

Fact: Everything we have comes from God.

- There isn't anything we own that we did not receive from God.

- Yet, we humans boastfully live as though we had anything to do with our genetics or privileges at all. When they are stripped away, we resent being stripped of our "rights."

- Having wealth can lead to arrogance and misplaced dependencies—putting your hope in wealth and what it provides for you. Instead, you should firmly plant your hope in God regardless of what He provides for you. *1 Timothy 6:17*

Fact: What we have is not a measure of our godliness or our faith.

- How God chooses to provide for you or me at any time in our lives is His sovereign choice. We are to give ourselves first to Him and trust Him with our daily needs as we do the work He gives us to do. *Philippians 4:12-13*

- Trusting God to take care of you and me in whatever manner He chooses is something we have to learn in our pursuit of godliness. Someone once told me that God is in the human development business. Christians having needs is part of God's plan.

- When God removes our comforts and strips away our support, we cry "help," give up our self-sufficiency, and actually begin to depend on God and think of Him as God Almighty— as essential to our lives, not just an appendage.

Fact: God determines our provision—the how, when, and why

- Most of the time, God's provision is going to come through people, not miraculously appear from the sky.

- It's okay to pray for prosperity for your business. Just remember that God chooses how He provides for His own. We must trust whatever manner He chooses. *Jeremiah 29:7*

Fact: It belongs to God. Hold onto it loosely.

- Adorning yourself with godliness means not putting your hope in wealth which is so uncertain. *1 Timothy 6:17*

- When we know Him and are devoted to Him, we can know that His every action is for a purpose that is goodness to us.

LESSON #2: GOD'S PROVISION IS ALWAYS ENOUGH. RECEIVE IT GRATEFULLY.

- The Bible says in 1 Timothy 6:8 that we should be grateful for whatever God provides. When you have the Lord's provision, you lack nothing that you need at this time in your life. Rejoice at what you have instead of complaining about what you don't have.

- During Jesus' ministry, He didn't have a 10,000 square-foot house and servants to care for His needs. God continually provided for Him, often through women. And, it was enough.

LESSON #3: GOD'S PROVISION IS MEANT TO BE SHARED. GIVE IT GENEROUSLY.

- Out of the most severe trial, the Philippians' overflowing joy and their extreme poverty welled up in rich generosity. They gave themselves first to the Lord in keeping with God's will. *2 Corinthians 8:1-5*

- God's riches to us are supplied through us to meet another's needs. Some of the Ephesians were very rich in both the Gospel and in material possessions. The command to them, and to us, in 1 Timothy 6:18-19 is to be generous and willing to share.

- That requires trusting God, not having plenty. How you handle whatever provision God gives you reveals how you much you are adorning yourself with godliness regarding money.

  "It is not what you'd do with a million, if riches should ever be your lot. But what you are doing at present with the dollar and a quarter you've got."

- Godliness is viewing God's provision as something belonging to Him and not to be hoarded for a future use that may never come. *Luke 12:20-21*

- Gratefully receiving and generously giving comes from the overflowing joy of knowing Jesus Christ and what He's doing in your life. Whether you are the receiver or the giver, how you do both should be different than what the world does.

Godliness begins with devotion to God. When you are devoted to Him, you view His provision as belonging to Him. You enjoy what He provides with contentment. You put your hope in God rather than wealth as a protection from falling into the traps of those whose hope is in getting rich however you can. By generously sharing with others the very riches He gives to you, you lay up treasure for yourself in heaven as others see your godliness and are drawn to believe in the God you love and know. And, all of that brings glory to the same God who is the object of your worship. It's a win/win.

Let Jesus satisfy your heart with such love for God that you will want to live a life that pleases Him.

9: Being Known by Your Actions

Titus 1:1-16

DAY ONE STUDY—GET THE BIG PICTURE

Ask the Lord Jesus to teach you through His Word.

Historical Insight: Who was Titus? Titus was a Greek from Antioch (Syria), the son of Gentile parents, who had been with Paul since the apostle's early ministry. He accompanied Paul and Barnabas to Jerusalem to show the apostles and other Jewish believers how a Greek, uncircumcised non-Jew could love God just as much as they did. Titus represented all the other non-Jewish people who became Christians and were completely accepted by God through their faith in Jesus Christ—like most of us.

Titus also served as Paul's special representative to the Corinthian church during Paul's third missionary journey. He carried the "severe letter" to that church from Ephesus and met Paul in Macedonia to give a good report about the church. Titus was also the leader of the group of men whom Paul sent to the churches in Macedonia and Achaia, to pick up the collection for the poor saints in Jerusalem.

After Paul was released from the Roman prison where he had been for two years, he and Titus traveled to Crete. Crete is an island in the Mediterranean Sea south of Greece. It had a large population of Jews at the time of Paul. We don't know exactly when the gospel first took root in Crete. Jews from Crete had been in the crowd that listened to Peter preach on the day of Pentecost (Acts 2:11). At least one church existed there before Paul and Titus visited. Soon there were enough believers to start churches in several towns. Paul wanted to visit the church in Corinth so he left Titus in Crete to continue teaching the new Christians and to appoint church leaders for each new church. Paul wrote this letter to Titus soon after writing 1 Timothy, probably while Paul was in Macedonia on his way to Nicopolis (modern Albania).

Later, someone came to replace Titus in Crete so he could rejoin Paul, likely in Nicopolis. When Paul was arrested again and brought to the dungeon in Rome, Titus remained near for a time until Paul sent him to Dalmatia (also in modern Albania). According to ancient tradition, Titus returned to Crete in his old age, where he died and was buried at the age of 94.

What does it say?

You read the letter called Titus in Lesson One. To refresh your memory, read the letter again at one sitting. It will take about 7 minutes. You can read the letter in any translation of the Bible you choose. Remember that a copy of Titus (NIV translation) is included in this study guide before Lesson One. Look again for references to godliness and God-pleasing behavior that you might have missed the first time. Then, answer the questions below.

1. What grabbed your attention this time from your reading of the letter?

2. What subjects did you see in this letter that you also read in 1 Timothy?

Ask the Lord to show you what He wants you to learn through your study of Titus.

DAY TWO STUDY—GET THE BIG PICTURE

Ask the Lord Jesus to teach you through His Word.

What does the Bible say?

Read Titus chapter 1 below (NIV). Use your own method (colored pencils, lines, shapes) to mark 1) anything that grabs your attention, 2) words you want to understand, and 3) topics you have already seen in 1 Timothy. Draw arrows between thoughts that connect. Put a star ✸ next to anything you think relates to godliness.

1 *¹ Paul, a servant of God and an apostle of Jesus Christ to further the faith of God's elect and their knowledge of the truth that leads to godliness— ² in the hope of eternal life, which God, who does not lie, promised before the beginning of time, ³ and which now at his appointed season he has brought to light through the preaching entrusted to me by the command of God our Savior,*

⁴ To Titus, my true son in our common faith: Grace and peace from God the Father and Christ Jesus our Savior.

⁵ The reason I left you in Crete was that you might put in order what was left unfinished and appoint elders in every town, as I directed you. ⁶ An elder must be blameless, faithful to his wife, a man whose children believe and are not open to the charge of being wild and disobedient. ⁷ Since an overseer manages God's household, he must be blameless—not overbearing, not quick-tempered, not given to drunkenness, not violent, not pursuing dishonest gain. ⁸ Rather, he must be hospitable, one who loves what is good, who is self-controlled, upright, holy and disciplined. ⁹ He must hold firmly to the trustworthy message as it has been taught, so that he can encourage others by sound doctrine and refute those who oppose it.

¹⁰ For there are many rebellious people, full of meaningless talk and deception, especially those of the circumcision group. ¹¹ They must be silenced, because they are disrupting whole households by teaching things they ought not to teach—and that for the sake of dishonest gain. ¹² One of Crete's own prophets has said it: "Cretans are always liars, evil brutes, lazy gluttons." ¹³ This saying is true. Therefore rebuke them sharply, so that they will be sound in the faith ¹⁴ and will pay no attention to Jewish myths or to the merely human commands of those who reject the truth. ¹⁵ To the pure, all things are pure, but to those who are corrupted and do not believe, nothing is pure. In fact, both their minds and consciences are corrupted. ¹⁶ They claim to know God, but by their actions they deny him. They are detestable, disobedient and unfit for doing anything good.

3. What grabbed your attention from Titus 1:1-16?

4. What verses or specific words do you want to understand better?

5. What words or phrases are repeated in this passage? Give verses.

6. What topics (if any) in this passage have we studied in previous lessons? Give verses.

7. What verses illustrate or help you understand what godliness looks like?

8. ***Adorn yourself with godliness:*** From this lesson's passage (Titus 1:1-16), choose one verse to dwell upon all week long. Write it in the space below. Ask God to teach you through this verse.

Respond to the Lord about what you learned today.

DAY THREE STUDY

Read Titus 1:1-16. Ask the Lord Jesus to teach you through His Word.

We will focus on vv. 1-5 in this session.

What does it mean?

9. How did Paul describe himself in v. 1?

Focus on the Meaning: Paul considered himself a slave or servant of his Lord Jesus Christ. He used the word *doulos*. In the Jewish culture, a *doulos* was someone who had been freed from slavery but now voluntarily commits himself to serve a master he loves and respects. That's what Jesus desires from us. That we would not only choose to serve Him as master but remain loyal to Him as our master every day.

10. "Bondservant" was Paul's relationship to God. "Apostle" was his role in God's plan. Paul next described his purpose in v. 1 and end of v. 2. What is it?

11. Our knowledge of the truth of God should lead to godliness (v. 1). Based on what you have learned so far in this study, what is the definition of godliness?

12. **Deeper Discoveries (optional):** Compare how Paul described himself in Titus 1:1 with how he described himself in the other 12 letters he wrote. The chronological order would be this: Galatians, 1 Thessalonians, 2 Thessalonians, 1 Corinthians, Romans, 2 Corinthians, Ephesians, Philippians, Colossians, Philemon, 1 Timothy, and 2 Timothy. What do you learn?

Paul addressed this letter to Titus, his "true son in the common faith." This is similar to how he addressed Timothy in 1 Timothy 1:2. Paul was the spiritual father of both men, meaning he had led both to Christ and discipled them. Then, Paul greeted everyone with "grace and peace from God the Father and Christ Jesus our Savior.

> **Focus on the Meaning:** Paul usually began his letters with the greeting "grace and peace to you." Grace (Greek, *charis*) was a common greeting among the Greeks, and peace (Hebrew, *shalom*) was a common greeting among Jews. Paul combined them together, elevating their meaning. Through His grace offered in the gospel, every believer received peace with God by faith in Christ.

13. Paul often introduced a letter with comments relevant to the letter's message.

- On what is our faith resting and why (v. 2)?

- What did God do to reveal His promise (v. 3)?

> **Scriptural Insight:** God revealed His plan not only through Paul but also through every other person sent out to share the gospel since the day of Pentecost—Peter, Philip, Barnabas, Silas, and all the way down to the one who shared it with you.

- Based upon what you read in vv. 1-3, what would you expect to see as Paul's emphasis in this letter?

14. For what two purposes did Paul send Titus to Crete (v. 5)?

> **Focus on the Meaning:** Titus, like Timothy, served as the agent of an apostle so he had apostolic authority. He was in a position of authority over the other local Christians.

15. ***Deeper Discoveries (optional):*** Titus 1:1 speaks of the truth that leads to godliness.

- Read the following passages. John 8:31-32; 14:6; 17:1-8, 17. Summarize what Jesus says is "truth."

- Then, read John 14:16-18; 16:13-14; and 1 Corinthians 2:10-16. How does the believer continue to discern truth?

What application will you make to adorn yourself with godliness?

16. Knowledge of the truth of God should lead to living a life adorned with godliness. We have already seen a lot of examples of what godliness looks like through our study of 1 Timothy.

- Are you taking what you learn in God's Word and obediently trying to apply it in your life?

- What are you trusting God to do in your life right now in regards to adorning yourself with a specific godly attitude or behavior?

Respond to the Lord about what you learned today.

DAY FOUR STUDY

Read Titus 1:1-16. Ask the Lord Jesus to teach you through His Word.

We will focus on vv. 6-16 in this session.

> **Historical Insight:** The Cretan character was proverbial in the ancient world. In Greek, to "Cretanize" meant to lie. The writer that Paul mentioned in verse 12 was Epimenides, a Cretan philosopher of the sixth century B.C. Most educated men of Paul's day had to study Epimenides. (*Titus Lifechange Series Bible Study*)

What does it mean?

God is a God of order (1 Corinthians 14:33). The orderliness of the church promotes and enhances people coming to the knowledge of the truth that leads to godliness (v. 1).

> **Think About It:** Godliness is the intended result of the gospel. Godliness that comes through the message about Jesus Christ is what the church supports and displays to the world. The responsibility of the church leadership is to correct and convict those who speak against godliness (1:9) and to counteract the influence of evil people. This is done by revealing God's truth.

Knowing truth should lead to knowing God and loving Him. From this springs obedience from the heart. Godliness is not conformity. It is devotion to a God who loves you dearly so that you want to live a life that pleases Him. Adorning yourself with godliness is for Him first then for yourself and for others.

17. Review the qualifications of elders in Titus 1:6-9. In vv. 6-7, Paul used the character trait "blameless" twice. "Blameless" does not mean sinless. It means "above reproach" regarding any character or conduct that would bring justifiable criticism on him or the church.

    • Considering what Paul said about the reputation of the Cretans in v. 12, why was it important that the leaders must be blameless or above reproach?

    • What qualifications for elder (vv. 6-9) contrast with the accepted behavior of the Cretan culture (v. 12)?

> **Scriptural Insight:** Regarding v. 6: We saw in 1 Timothy 3 that the godly elder must be able to lead his own household well. Concerning children, the Greek word describing them means "faithful" thus describing children who are faithful in honoring their parents (see Exodus 20:12). The decision to believe in Christ belongs to the child. Even the best Christian parent cannot guarantee it. So this phrase likely means that the elder's children are **faithful** in obeying the head of the house (see 1 Timothy 3:4) or trustworthy in honoring their parents as adults.

- As a manager (steward) of God's household (v. 7), what must the godly elder be able to do for his congregation (v. 9)?

- Of the qualifications for elders in vv. 6-9, which ones would also be godly adornment for every Christian, not just those in leadership?

18. Elders must be able to encourage others by sound doctrine and refute those who oppose it. Notice that what we see in Titus regarding false teaching and false teachers is not much different from what we saw in 1 Timothy or could see in any other New Testament letter. In Crete, rebellious people were opposing sound doctrine for the purpose of dishonest gain. The motive is always greed and power.

- Paul gave a series of instructions to negate the influence of false teachers. What actions should Titus (and church leaders) take? See also Titus 3:9-10.

- Why must the false teachers be silenced (v. 11)?

- What is the hope after they are rebuked (vv. 12-13)?

- How are those who do not believe in Christ described (vv. 15-16)?

Scriptural Insight: To Christians, who have been purified by the atoning death of Christ, "everything God created is good, and nothing is to be rejected if it is received with thanksgiving" (1 Timothy 4:4). Unbelievers, especially ascetics [or legalists] with unbiblical scruples against certain foods, marriage and the like, do not enjoy the freedom of true Christians, who receive all God's creation with thanksgiving. Instead, they set up arbitrary, man-made prohibitions against what they consider to be impure. The principle of this verse does not conflict with the many NT teachings against practices that are morally and spiritually wrong. (*NIV Study Bible*, note on Titus 1:15, p. 1852)

19. ***Deeper Discoveries (optional):*** Compare what Paul says about false teachers to what Jesus says about the Pharisees in Mark 7:5-13 and Luke 11:42-44. How are the false teachers and Pharisees alike? How are they different?

20. Review Titus 1:16. Read also 2 Timothy 3:5 for a similar statement.

   • How can a person claims to know God live a life that is actually denying God? How would you recognize it?

   • How is this behavior the opposite of godliness? Consider our definition of godliness.

What application will you make to adorn yourself with godliness?

21. Consider the culture in which you live. What three words would you use to describe the predominant characteristics of the people? As a Christian, what three displays of godliness in your life are the opposite of those you just wrote?

22. Have you allowed any influences in your life that are ruining your household, which would include anyone over which you have influence (Titus 1:11)? What will you do to "silence" those corrupting influences so that your daily actions would reflect your relationship with God rather than deny Him (v. 16)?

23. Reflect on Titus 1:16. Do your daily actions deny or reflect God? Ask God to help you recognize where your actions deny Him, repent of that sin, and depend on Christ to replace that bad behavior with godliness instead.

24. In Lesson Nine, we saw several evidences of godliness displayed—devotion to God expressed in a life pleasing to Him. Feel free to add to the list in the chart below. Choose one example of godliness from this passage. Ask the Lord Jesus to give you a desire for that in your life and to adorn you with that. He has the power to make it happen.

Verse(s)	What godliness looks like
v. 8	Be hospitable, a lover of what is good, self-controlled, upright, holy and disciplined.
v. 9	Hold firmly to the truth
v. 9	Encourage others with the truth
v. 14	Pay no attention to those who are rebellious and reject the truth
v. 16	Having actions that are consistent with your claim to know God

Respond to the Lord about what you learned today.

Recommended: Listen to the podcast "Godliness Leaves No Room for Rebelliousness" after doing this lesson to reinforce what you have learned. Use the following listener guide.

Godliness Leaves No Room for Rebelliousness

THE INFLUENCE OF THE REBELLIOUS

"For there are many rebellious people, full of meaningless talk and deception, especially those of the circumcision group. They must be silenced, because they are disrupting whole households by teaching things they ought not to teach—and that for the sake of dishonest gain. ... They claim to know God, but by their actions they deny Him." (Titus 1:10-11,16)

- Influential fakers were acting religious, playing a part to gain influence and power over genuine Christians. According to the Bible, such influential fakers were and are, "detestable, disobedient and unfit for doing anything good."

- Why do people who have tasted the goodness of the Gospel rebel against it? We can recognize three different reasons why someone would give up on the Gospel and go their own way. I covered the first one in the podcast for Lesson 5. Some abandon the faith because they are turned off by the hypocrisy of legalism and discouraged by the hopelessness of legalism. But, we can see two other situations that feed rebelliousness.

DISAPPOINTMENT IN GOD'S ANSWER TO A SPECIFIC PRAYER FEEDS REBELLIOUSNESS.

- Human nature has not changed one whit over the millennia of recorded history. Nations, jobs, and life experiences have changed. But, human responses to authority, hardships, fellow humans, and God have not changed. *Jeremiah 42:3,6*

- People want their own way, and they want God's blessing on them to do that. When God doesn't answer a prayer a certain way, they turn their backs on God. We more quickly say, "My will be done" than we say, "Your will be done, O Lord."

- So, we hold onto expectations of what we want. When God chooses a different answer, we don't like it. We don't trust His goodness, and we run away from Him instead, usually in anger. So, disappointment in how God answers a specific prayer feeds rebelliousness.

- What is the answer? Trust God. Trust His goodness in whatever He chooses to do. It will always turn out better than anything you plan. Don't let disappointment in God's answer to a specific prayer feed rebelliousness in you.

HANGING ON TO A FAVORITE SIN FEEDS REBELLIOUSNESS.

- Whenever we read about a professing Christian who claims to no longer believe in Christ, often buried in the story is sinful behavior they don't want to give up. *Jeremiah 44:4, 16-17*

- People who are in rebellion like to hang onto their rebellion against God and encourage others to do the same. Having honest doubts and questions that you are willing to explore is not sin. Rebellion against God is sin.

- As long as you live in your earthly body, you will be tempted to sin. Don't let yourself hang onto a favorite sin so that it feeds rebelliousness in you.

- If you are a Christian, let it go. Here's how to deal with recognized sin in your life:
  - ✓ Remember that your identity is child of God.
  - ✓ Agree with God that you've sinned against Him and mourn your sin.
  - ✓ Depend on the Holy Spirit to help you obey God in the future. Ask His help to overcome that sin, to let it go.
  - ✓ Trust in Him to help you overcome the consequences of any sinful choices that you've made and to do so in a way that brings glory to Him.
  - ✓ That's living a life that pleases the Lord in every way. That will lead to restored godliness in your life.

CONCLUSION

- In response to those in rebellion against God, stop enabling them. Don't buy their products. Don't let their words into your homes. Pray for the Holy Spirit to convict them of their sin of rebellion and turn to the God of forgiveness and complete renewal. *Titus 1:11*

- Stay devoted to God even when you don't get your way or what you want to happen. He is bigger than any of your plans. Trust Him.

Let Jesus satisfy your heart with such love for God that you will want to live a life that pleases Him.

10: Adorn Yourself with Godliness in Relationships

Titus 2:1-15

DAY ONE STUDY—GET THE BIG PICTURE

Ask the Lord Jesus to teach you through His Word.

What does the Bible say?

Read the Bible passage below (NIV) including verses from the last lesson. Use your own method (colored pencils, lines, shapes) to mark 1) anything that grabs your attention, 2) words you want to understand, and 3) topics you have seen before in this letter. Draw arrows between thoughts that connect. Put a star ✱ next to anything you think relates to godliness.

1 *[10] For there are many rebellious people, full of meaningless talk and deception, especially those of the circumcision group. [11] They must be silenced, because they are disrupting whole households by teaching things they ought not to teach—and that for the sake of dishonest gain. [12] One of Crete's own prophets has said it: "Cretans are always liars, evil brutes, lazy gluttons." [13] This saying is true. Therefore rebuke them sharply, so that they will be sound in the faith [14] and will pay no attention to Jewish myths or to the merely human commands of those who reject the truth. [15] To the pure, all things are pure, but to those who are corrupted and do not believe, nothing is pure. In fact, both their minds and consciences are corrupted. [16] They claim to know God, but by their actions they deny him. They are detestable, disobedient and unfit for doing anything good.*

2 *[1] You, however, must teach what is appropriate to sound doctrine. [2] Teach the older men to be temperate, worthy of respect, self-controlled, and sound in faith, in love and in endurance.*

[3] Likewise, teach the older women to be reverent in the way they live, not to be slanderers or addicted to much wine, but to teach what is good. [4] Then they can urge the younger women to love their husbands and children, [5] to be self-controlled and pure, to be busy at home, to be kind, and to be subject to their husbands, so that no one will malign the word of God.

[6] Similarly, encourage the young men to be self-controlled. [7] In everything set them an example by doing what is good. In your teaching show integrity, seriousness [8] and soundness of speech that cannot be condemned, so that those who oppose you may be ashamed because they have nothing bad to say about us.

[9] Teach slaves to be subject to their masters in everything, to try to please them, not to talk back to them, [10] and not to steal from them, but to show that they can be fully trusted, so that in every way they will make the teaching about God our Savior attractive.

[11] For the grace of God has appeared that offers salvation to all people. [12] It teaches us to say "No" to ungodliness and worldly passions, and to live self-controlled, upright and godly lives in this present age, [13] while we wait for the blessed hope—the appearing of the glory of our great God and Savior, Jesus Christ, [14] who gave himself for us to redeem us from all wickedness and to purify for himself a people that are his very own, eager to do what is good.

[15] These, then, are the things you should teach. Encourage and rebuke with all authority. Do not let anyone despise you.

1. What grabbed your attention from Titus 2:1-15?

2. What verses or specific words do you want to understand better?

3. What words or phrases are repeated in this passage? Give verses.

4. What topics (if any) in this passage have we studied in previous lessons? Give verses.

5. What verses illustrate or help you understand what godliness looks like?

6. ***Adorn yourself with godliness:*** From this lesson's passage (Titus 2:1-15), choose one verse to dwell upon all week long. Write it in the space below. Ask God to teach you through this verse.

Respond to the Lord about what you learned today.

DAY TWO STUDY

Read Titus 2:1-15. Ask the Lord Jesus to teach you through His Word.

We will focus on vv. 1-6 in this session.

What does it mean?

In the last lesson, we studied the instructions to Titus about false teachers. To counter their influence, Titus must continue to teach what is in accord with sound doctrine (v. 1). This was essential for him to do because the false teachers were ruining whole households with their polluted (corrupted) teaching. Grasping truth is necessary for every Christian, male or female, to recognize deceivers and overcome the error that they teach. Having godly older men and women modeling the truth for the younger ones is necessary in every church.

> **Scriptural Insight:** We human beings seem to be imitative by nature. We need models; they give us direction, challenge and inspiration. Paul did not hesitate to offer himself, as an apostle, for the churches to imitate. "Follow my example," he wrote, "as I follow the example of Christ" (1 Corinthians 11:1). And Paul expected both Timothy and Titus to provide a model, which the church [members] could follow. (John Stott, *Fighting the Good Fight*, p. 50)

Verses 2-6 describe the adornment of godliness each member of the household of God should have that was appropriate for them as individuals and in their relationships with others. In this way, they would behave consistently with what they profess to believe (opposite of Titus 1:16) and be good examples for others.

> **Historical Insight:** Except for older widows, men and women of that culture normally had spouses and children. These verses do not teach that being married and having children are required for godliness. In that culture, older men and women would have been over 40. Younger men and women would have been under 40.

7. Instructions to men:

    • What specific aspects of godliness are the older men to be taught to display in their lives (v. 2)?

    • What specific aspects of godliness are the younger men to be taught to display in their lives (v. 6 and first part of v. 7)?

Instructions to women: Obviously, God has outlined a specific plan for older women to encourage and disciple younger women in the church. The discipling is the duty of the older women who are qualified to do so by position, character, and life experience.

8. Older women:

- What specific aspects of godliness are the older women to be taught to display in their lives (v. 3)? Compare these descriptions with what you learned about female deacons in 1 Timothy 3:11.

- "To be reverent in the way they live" means behavior suitable to one in whom Jesus lives. The word refers to a priestess serving in the temple of her God. Our bodies are the temple of God who dwells within us. Everything we do in life is service to Him, reflecting our devotion to Him. What would that look like in a woman's life?

- "To teach what is good" refers to teaching right from wrong, truth about God and about what God desires. How do you learn that so you can teach it to others?

9. Younger women:

- What specific aspects of godliness are the younger women to be taught to display in their lives (vv. 4-5)? Note: the older women should have these displayed in their lives as well in order to mentor the younger ones. ☺

From the Greek: The underlying Greek word translated "urge" (other translations say "train" or "encourage") means to restore one to her senses; to disciple; to hold one to her duty; to reprove firmly but kindly, to remind or advise about something forgotten or disregarded.

- Why would younger women need to be "urged" in the specifics mentioned in Titus 2:4-5?

10. What would be the advantages of this kind of mentoring relationship?

Focus on the Meaning: We have bought into the notion that older people have had their day of usefulness and ought to make way for the young. But the principle here is quite the opposite. With age and experience come wisdom, and many older women have discovered secrets of godly living in relation to their husbands, children and neighbors, and in the work place that could save younger women a lot of unnecessary grief. And when the unavoidable trials come to the young woman, who better to guide her through than an older sister who has been through it before? (*Dr. Constable's Notes on Tits 2020 Edition,* pp. 26-27)

11. The word "self-controlled" is used 3 times in Titus 2:2-6, and again in v. 12. The original Greek word means primarily "of sound mind, sane, in one's senses." Its secondary meaning is "curbing one's desires and impulses, self-controlled, temperate." In other words, the word refers first of all to right thinking then to behavior that results from right thinking.

- Read Romans 12:2-3. In the pursuit of godliness, why is right thinking so important?

- What could happen when you try to force correct behavior upon someone without "renewing the mind" with truth that leads to right thinking?

12. What is the purpose of teaching men and women of all ages to display all of those aspects of godliness in their lives? See Titus 1:16 and 2:5.

What application will you make to adorn yourself with godliness?

> **Focus on the Meaning:** Mentoring is someone older in the Lord helping someone younger in the Lord understand and apply biblical truth to everyday life. It is the "how" of discipling.

13. In Titus 2:4, the older women are given the responsibility of mentoring the younger women to be sensible, sane and sober-minded. This involves the cultivation of sound judgment and prudence in your own life.

- If you are an older woman, how are you cultivating sound judgment in your life right now?

- What else can you give to a relationship with a woman who is younger or younger in the Lord?

- Ask the Lord to give you someone to mentor / disciple as you pursue godliness.

14. If you are a younger woman:

- In what areas do you need help from an older woman or someone older in the Lord?

- What can you give to a relationship with an older woman?

- Ask the Lord to give you someone to mentor / disciple or to mentor / disciple you as you pursue godliness.

Respond to the Lord about what you learned today.

DAY THREE STUDY

Read Titus 2:1-15. Ask the Lord Jesus to teach you through His Word.

We will focus on vv. 7-10 in this session.

What does it mean?

Paul's counsel to Titus in vv. 7-8 is similar to what he gave to Timothy (1 Timothy 4:12, 15). Set an example by teaching what is sound and doing what is good.

15. Why is the example of a leader or teacher so important…?

  - To the local church—

  - To the community—

16. ***Deeper Discoveries (optional):*** Read 2 Thessalonians 3:6-9 and 1 Peter 2:21 to see what the Bible has to say about setting a good example. What do you learn?

17. Go back to Lesson 7 Day Three Study to review what you learned about slavery in Paul's day. Every Christian slave or master would fit into the categories of older men, younger men, older women, and younger women that we find in Titus 2:2-6. All were to adorn themselves with godliness as individuals. The counsel for the master / slave relationship was in the context of a work place. In Titus 2:9-10 (first part), what counsel did Paul give to those under the yoke of slavery?

> **Historical Insight:** The Roman statesman Cicero complained that the Cretans did not consider it immoral to steal.

Why adorn ourselves with godliness? We do it first for God the Father and our Lord Jesus Christ because of our love for them and gratitude for what they have done for our salvation (1 Timothy 4:10). We adorn ourselves with godliness for ourselves and our fellow Christians because godly behavior is good for us in every way (1 Timothy 6:6, 19; Titus 2:11-13).

18. Titus 2:10 gives another reason. Read the last part of Titus 2:10 in different translations to help in understanding it.

- For what other reason should we adorn ourselves with godliness?

- How does adorning ourselves with godliness do this?

> **Think About It:** Paul commanded this of slaves (v. 10). If they could do it, all others can. To adorn means to set forth attractively. I heard it said this way, "The burden is not on the world to recognize our faith. The burden is on us to demonstrate a life of dependency on Christ who is the real thing." (Tim Stevenson, sermon notes on Titus 2:11-3:7, 10/19/2003)

What application will you make to adorn yourself with godliness?

19. Think of people who have had the greatest effect on your life. In what ways did they influence you for good?

20. "Because I told you" worked as an incentive to do something when we were young children and accepted everything our parents told us. But, as we grew into teenagers, it was no longer a sufficient reason for changing our actions. We wanted to know why and needed greater incentive. What motivates you to change your behavior now? What should be your motivation to adorn yourself with godliness?

Respond to the Lord about what you learned today.

DAY FOUR STUDY

Read Titus 2:1-15. Ask the Lord Jesus to teach you through His Word.

We will focus on vv. 11-15 in this session.

What does it say?

21. Answer the questions below based on what is in the text.

For the grace of God has appeared to do what (v. 11)?

The grace of God teaches us to say "No" to what (v. 12, first part)?

The grace of God teaches us to do what (v. 12, second part)?

While we wait for what (v. 13)?

Jesus Christ gave Himself for us to do what (v. 14)?

What should Titus do and not do (v. 15)?

What does it mean?

> **Focus on the Meaning:** Grace is commonly defined as "unmerited favor, an undeserved gift." It is God's gift to an undeserving humanity. God gives His grace to us in the gospel of Jesus Christ because of His great love and mercy (Ephesians 2:4-7).

Paul repeatedly affirmed the importance of God's grace. God offered a solution to our sin problem. We humans have a spiritual problem that can be compared to death caused by a fatal disease. It's a two-fold problem. Sin is the disease. Romans 3:23 says that all have sinned and fallen short of the glory of God. Everyone has the sin disease. And, death is the result of the disease. We are born spiritually dead sinners. Our double whammy problem demanded a two-fold solution. The great news is that God acted on our behalf.

- For the problem of sin, people need sin to be removed and replaced with righteousness. *God's answer is Christ's death on the cross.* Because of His finished work on the cross, we can now be cured of the disease.

- For the problem of death, people need the restoration of life. *God's answer is Christ's resurrection.* We can now be given life that is forever.

The Gospel message included the answer to both spiritual problems. We are saved from the consequences of our sins. And, we are given the life of Christ in us to enable us to live to please God from the moment we receive that salvation.

22. Knowing we have the grace of God through our faith in Jesus Christ, and appreciating that truth,

- How would that teach us to say "No" to ungodliness and worldly passions?

- How would that teach us to live godly lives in this present age, in the midst of corrupt culture and people? Note: "Godly" (adjective) and "godliness" (noun) mean the same thing.

- In what ways is Christ our blessed hope?

Focus on the Meaning: Anyone understanding the grace of God should respond to that grace with greater love for God and gratitude to Him for all that He has done. Grace is a prime motivator for many aspects of life change including, but not limited to, a desire to get to know God and His Word, a desire to serve, the joy of being with other believers, graciousness to others, and compassion on a lost world. This is "graceful living" leading to a life of freedom and joy.

23. The "Deeper Discoveries" question in Lesson Eight Day Two Study covered the references to Christ's appearing to claim His own from this earth so that we will be with Him from then on. How would the hope of Christ's coming for us be an encouragement to live self-controlled, upright, and godly lives today while we are waiting?

24. You read in Titus 2:14 that Jesus Christ gave Himself for us to redeem us. Redemption means that you are "purchased out of bondage to sin and released into freedom to serve God." Every human born on this planet is born into bondage, not just those living in slavery. Based on the following verses, we are born in bondage to what?

- John 8:34—

- Colossians 1:13—

Romans chapter 6 describes how the slave master "sin" calls the shots. Obedience comes too easily. It's a trap. The readers of the New Testament were very familiar with the hopelessness of being owned by a slave master. The only two ways out of the miserable cycle were either death or being bought by someone who would set you free. Jesus did that for you. You are released from that trap of slavery to sin the moment you trust in Jesus Christ. The Bible calls this "redemption."

25. Jesus came to set us free.

- Read Mark 10:45. What did Jesus declare about His purpose?

- Read Ephesians 1:7 and 1 Peter 1:18-19, how are we redeemed?

- According to Titus 2:13-14, from what did Jesus Christ redeem us?

- What did Christ want to accomplish through our redemption?

Think About It: Since Jesus Christ has paid a full ransom price, the believer is a possession of God and is secure in freedom until his complete redemption of the body is accomplished. That takes place at Christ's appearing (v. 13). To summarize this section (vv. 11-14), "the grace of God" should result in the Christian's present commitment to deny what God detests and to pursue what God values. For more explanation about redemption, check out my blog series, "The Gospel: God's Cure for Our Fatal Sin Disease" on melanienewton.com.

26. ***Deeper Discoveries (optional):*** Read Romans 6:15-23. This passage contrasts the results of the life serving sin with that of serving God. Put the descriptions under the headings below.

Slavery to sin leads to what results?   *Serving God leads to what results?*

What application will you make to adorn yourself with godliness?

27. You have been freed from a life of slavery to sin. Your freedom makes it possible for you to offer yourself to God and His righteousness instead. The rewards are godliness that reflects a heart that is obedient to God.

    - Are you experiencing the freedom from slavery to sin in your life right now? If not, do you have confidence that you do not have to listen to the voice of your old slave master sin?

    - You have a new master with greater power living inside of you, the Spirit of God Himself, who can give you freedom from any entrapping sin. Claim that freedom now. Choose to obey the Spirit inside you who will lead you and empower you to say "no" to ungodliness and worldly passions.

28. In Lesson Ten, we saw several evidences of godliness displayed—devotion to God expressed in a life pleasing to Him. Feel free to add to the list in the chart below. Choose one example of godliness from this passage. Ask the Lord Jesus to give you a desire for that in your life and to adorn you with that. He has the power to make it happen.

Verse(s)	What godliness looks like
v. 3	*Be reverent in the way that you live.*
v. 3	*Teach what is good.*
vv. 4-5	*Urge others to be godly in their relationships and behavior.*
vv. 7, 14	*Set an example of / be eager for doing what is good.*
v. 10	*In everything, make the teaching about God our Savior attractive to outsiders.*
v. 12	*Say "No" to ungodliness and worldly passions*
v. 12	*Live self-controlled, upright, and godly lives*
v. 13	*Eagerly wait for Christ's appearing*

Respond to the Lord about what you learned today.

Recommended: Listen to the podcast "Godliness Is Transferable from Woman to Woman" after doing this lesson to reinforce what you have learned. Use the following listener guide.

Godliness Is Transferable from Woman to Woman

THE NEED FOR MENTORS

- Some women today were raised by mothers who loved and served Jesus. Others might have come from a household where Jesus was a curse word. Lack of godly role models leaves many women confused about living as a Christian. Old habits are hard to break.

- The biblical remedy is sound teaching that leads to devotion to God so that you desire to live a life that pleases Him. That will lead you to desire godly relationships with other believers who can demonstrate godliness in their lives as examples for you to follow.

WHAT IS GOD'S PLAN?

- God gave to the older women the responsibility of discipling and counseling the younger women because they can do it better! Who else knows the mind and body of a woman better than another woman?

- An older woman is any woman who has more life experience or spiritual maturity than another woman.

- If you know Jesus Christ and expressed that love for Him through a life that is more godly than ungodly, then you are qualified because you have life experiences that are marketable skills in God's economy and make you very valuable to His service.

- What is the responsibility of the older woman? She needs to adorn herself with godliness so she has something to offer another woman.

BEING REVERENT IN THE WAY YOU LIVE

- The Greek word used in Titus 2:3 refers to a priestess serving in the temple of her God. Out of your devotion to God flows your daily work for God in everything—loving your family, caring for your homes, anything you do outside of your home, and serving in your church community.

- What are some ways that this reverence for God is expressed? The descriptions given in Titus 2:3 are similar to 1 Timothy 3:11. A woman who is reverent in the way she lives is worthy of respect because she is devoted to God. That she is not to be a slanderer or addicted to much wine is the same as not being a malicious talker and being temperate.

BEING ABLE TO TEACH WHAT IS GOOD.

- What is good? Sound doctrine. Christian truth. What devotion to God looks like. How that devotion is expressed in godly behavior. "What is good" means right from wrong, truth about God and about what God desires.

- Life's experiences teach us, if we are listening, to stay faithful to Christ as we are going through even the hardest times. Older women who have done that have so much to offer younger women. It is the Lord who makes you able to mentor someone else. We must rely on Him even in this simple way of woman-to-woman relationships.

- God in His infinite wisdom knows a woman should never "retire" from being committed to the development of quality life in others. A woman must feel needed and appreciated. God designed us that way and gave us an avenue to fill that need.

WHY WOULD THE YOUNGER WOMEN NEED WHAT THE OLDER WOMEN CAN OFFER?

- Women are affected by loneliness in our transitional society, confusion about life skills and relationships, and just plain old busyness.

- The older women are "to urge" the younger women. The original Greek word means "to restore one to her senses." So, the duty of older women is to help the younger women to be restored to their senses when they get overwhelmed.

- That same Greek word also means "to disciple." Discipling is someone older in the Lord helping someone younger in the Lord understand and apply biblical truth to everyday life. Mentoring is the "how" of discipling. Younger women don't just need to know some life skills, but they need to know how to develop that devotion to God for themselves. They need to see what godliness looks like in another woman. *1 Timothy 3:11*

- Older women and younger women should all seek to adorn themselves with godliness. The woman who is older in the Lord and has learned how to do that can show any woman who is younger in the Lord what godliness looks like.

WHERE DO YOU FIND EACH OTHER?

If you are an older woman wanting to mentor:

- Ask the Lord to give you a desire and opportunity to mentor someone for Him. Make yourself available to younger women, especially those with no family close by. Then, pay attention and come alongside her.

If you are a younger woman wanting a mentor:

- Ask the Lord to lead you to someone who will want to invest in you. Interact with older women. Befriend them. Listen to them. Ask one to disciple you.

Discipling someone else will lead you to rely on Him more than on yourself. And, that's always a good thing for anyone learning how to adorn herself with godliness.

Let Jesus satisfy your heart with such love for God that you will want to live a life that pleases Him.

11: Living in Response to God's Grace

Titus 3:1-15

DAY ONE STUDY—GET THE BIG PICTURE

Ask the Lord Jesus to teach you through His Word.

What does the Bible say?

Read the Bible passage below (NIV) including verses from the last lesson. Use your own method (colored pencils, lines, shapes) to mark 1) anything that grabs your attention, 2) words you want to understand, and 3) topics you have seen before in this letter. Draw arrows between thoughts that connect. Put a star ✱ next to anything you think relates to godliness.

2 *[11] For the grace of God has appeared that offers salvation to all people. [12] It teaches us to say "No" to ungodliness and worldly passions, and to live self-controlled, upright and godly lives in this present age, [13] while we wait for the blessed hope—the appearing of the glory of our great God and Savior, Jesus Christ, [14] who gave himself for us to redeem us from all wickedness and to purify for himself a people that are his very own, eager to do what is good.*

[15] These, then, are the things you should teach. Encourage and rebuke with all authority. Do not let anyone despise you.

3 *[1] Remind the people to be subject to rulers and authorities, to be obedient, to be ready to do whatever is good, [2] to slander no one, to be peaceable and considerate, and always to be gentle toward everyone.*

[3] At one time we too were foolish, disobedient, deceived and enslaved by all kinds of passions and pleasures. We lived in malice and envy, being hated and hating one another. [4] But when the kindness and love of God our Savior appeared, [5] he saved us, not because of righteous things we had done, but because of his mercy. He saved us through the washing of rebirth and renewal by the Holy Spirit, [6] whom he poured out on us generously through Jesus Christ our Savior, [7] so that, having been justified by his grace, we might become heirs having the hope of eternal life. [8] This is a trustworthy saying. And I want you to stress these things, so that those who have trusted in God may be careful to devote themselves to doing what is good. These things are excellent and profitable for everyone.

[9] But avoid foolish controversies and genealogies and arguments and quarrels about the law, because these are unprofitable and useless. [10] Warn a divisive person once, and then warn them a second time. After that, have nothing to do with them. [11] You may be sure that such people are warped and sinful; they are self-condemned.

[12] As soon as I send Artemas or Tychicus to you, do your best to come to me at Nicopolis, because I have decided to winter there. [13] Do everything you can to help Zenas the lawyer and Apollos on their way and see that they have everything they need. [14] Our people must learn to devote themselves to doing what is good, in order to provide for urgent needs and not live unproductive lives.

[15] Everyone with me sends you greetings. Greet those who love us in the faith. Grace be with you all.

1. What grabbed your attention from Titus 3:1-15?

2. What verses or specific words do you want to understand better?

3. What words or phrases are repeated in this passage? Give verses.

4. What topics (if any) in this passage have we studied in previous lessons? Give verses.

5. What verses illustrate or help you understand what godliness looks like?

6. ***Adorn yourself with godliness:*** From this lesson's passage (Titus 3:1-15), choose one verse to dwell upon all week long. Write it in the space below. Ask God to teach you through this verse.

Respond to the Lord about what you learned today.

DAY TWO STUDY

Read Titus 3:1-15. Ask the Lord Jesus to teach you through His Word.

We will focus on vv. 1-7 in this session.

What does it mean?

7. Titus 3:1-2 illustrates behaviors generally exhibited by one who understands God's grace. These are illustrations of adorning ourselves with godliness for every believer regardless of age, gender, or social status. To adorn yourself with godliness means to adorn yourself with the very character of God so that your life displays the beliefs you claim to profess.

- What seven "adornments" did Paul describe? Note: These same qualities are consistent throughout all of Paul's letters as well as those of Peter.

- In what ways would those specific adornments display the beliefs we claim to profess as believers?

Think About It: Where all around there is disrespect or indifference to those in authority, a Christian's respectful attitude and speech, backed up by good performance, will demonstrate that God's message of salvation produces positive, visible results. (*Dr. Constable's Notes on Titus 2020 Edition,* p. 32)

It always helps to remember what life was like before Christ came into our lives and what He did for us to change that. We will be looking at Titus 3:3-7 and Ephesians 2:1-12.

8. Our condition before Christ came into our lives:

- How does Titus 3:3 describe our lives apart from God?

- Read Ephesians 2:1-3, 11-12. What else was true about our existence before trusting in Christ?

9. What Christ did for us:

- What motivated God to do something for us (Titus 3:4 and first part of 3:5)?

- What does God do for everyone who puts their faith in His Son Jesus Christ (Titus 3:5-7)?

- Read Ephesians 2:4-9. What do these verses add to what you learned in Titus?

10. The role of the Holy Spirit as described in Titus 3:5 is both rebirth and renewal. These are combined in the word "regeneration" meaning "the restoration of life."

> **Focus on the Meaning:** Regeneration (Gr., *paliggenesia*) is the work of the Holy Spirit in salvation whereby He gives a new life and nature to the believing sinner at the moment of salvation. The new birth (John 3:1-16) is the beginning of this new nature that becomes a part of the believing sinner the instant he or she receives Christ. (Chuck Swindoll)

- How did Jesus describe this "regeneration" in John 3:3-6?

- What is revealed about this in Ephesians 2:4-5?

- As a result of being "born again," what is now true of us according to 2 Corinthians 5:17?

- What do Galatians 2:20 and Colossians 1:27 say about our new life in Christ?

11. Not only does the Holy Spirit wash us with rebirth and renewal, Titus 3:7 says we become heirs having the hope of eternal life. Titus 2:14 says that our blessed hope is the glorious appearing of Christ—being able to see Him as He is. How does knowing this give you hope as you live today?

12. *Deeper Discoveries (optional):* Of what are we heirs? Use a concordance to look up New Testament verses talking about our inheritance in Christ. What do you learn?

> **Think About It:** In the human setting, heirs don't inherit until the owner of the estate dies (though they may enjoy many benefits in the meantime). But in the spiritual realm the opposite occurs: We do not fully inherit until we have died; yet in this life we can experience many joys and benefits of being heirs of God. Our experience now is only a foretaste of what God has guaranteed to us in the future. *(Life Application Bible Commentary)*

What application will you make to adorn yourself with godliness?

13. Looking at Titus 3:1-2, are you still struggling with not being able to adorn yourself with any of those godly behaviors? Talk to Jesus about it.

- *If it is a lack of respect for authority:* Do a search for Bible verses / passages that teach you how to respect authority then choose to trust God and obey Him in that area.

- *If it is struggling to be obedient to one of God's commands:* Trust that He wants the best for you in that area of your life. Choose to obey because you love God and are grateful for what He has done for you.

- *If it is your tendency to slander people who disagree with you:* Read Philippians 2:1-11 and imitate Christ in your behavior and words.

Respond to the Lord about what you learned today.

DAY THREE STUDY

Read Titus 3:1-15. Ask the Lord Jesus to teach you through His Word.

We will focus on vv. 8-15 in this session.

What does it mean?

> **Scriptural Insight:** Paul once again said, "This is a trustworthy saying (v. 8)." We have seen this phrase 3 times already in 1 Timothy (1:15; 3:1; and 4:9). It is also found in 2 Timothy 2:11. This phrase refers to the factual statement directly before or after it. In this case (Titus 3:8), the trustworthy statement is the beautiful description of the Gospel found in Titus 3:4-7.

14. Read Titus 2:14; 3:1, 8, 14. Paul continually reminds believers to be devoted to doing what is good.

    * Look up the definition of devoted and write out what it means.

    * When you realize and appreciate what your trust in God accomplishes for you, and that you have been reborn and renewed by the Holy Spirit, why should this status motivate you to devote yourself to doing what is good?

    * How would devoting yourself to doing good be excellent and profitable for everyone? See also Titus 3:14.

    * What would be considered unprofitable and useless (v. 9)? See references to this elsewhere in 1 Timothy and Titus.

15. Regarding those who insist on doing what is described in v. 9,

    * What should Titus (or any ministry leader) do (v. 10)?

- What does resistance to correction reveal about them (v. 11)?

- How is this behavior the opposite of godliness?

16. What were Paul's instructions in vv. 12-13?

Historical Insight: Paul evidently intended to send either "Artemas" or "Tychicus" (2 Timothy 4:12) to take Titus' place in Crete. Paul wanted Titus to join him for the coming "winter" in Nicopolis, probably the [town] in Illyricum, that lay on the Adriatic coast of western Greece, opposite northern Italy. "Zenas" and "Apollos" (cf. Acts 18:24-19:1) were apparently in Crete with Titus, and planned to leave Crete for other places of ministry. They may have previously carried this letter from Paul to Titus. Zenas was evidently a converted Jewish lawyer who was an expert in the Mosaic Law, as the word "lawyer" (Gr. *nomikon*) means in the Gospels. Or, he could have been an expert in Greek or Roman law, in view of his Greek name. (*Dr. Constable's Notes on Titus 2020 Edition*, p. 43)

17. How did Paul end this letter (v. 15)?

Historical Insight: The last mention of Titus in the Bible indicates that he was with Paul during Paul's final Roman imprisonment. From Rome, Titus was sent to evangelize Dalmatia (2 Timothy 4:10), an area which later became known as Yugoslavia and is now called Serbia and Montenegro.

What application will you make to adorn yourself with godliness?

18. If salvation is based on our faith and God's grace and mercy, why should we be devoted to good deeds? See Ephesians 2:10 as well as all that you have learned through this study.

19. Review Titus 3:9-11. The context of these instructions is the church and, especially, for the church authorities. But, you can glean wisdom for your interactions with people outside the church as well.

- How can you avoid unprofitable, or empty, discussions and ensure healthy ones?

- In what situations or relationships could you apply vv. 10-11?

20. In Lesson Eleven, we saw several evidences of godliness displayed—devotion to God expressed in a life pleasing to Him. Feel free to add to the list in the chart below. Choose one example of godliness from this passage. Ask the Lord Jesus to give you a desire for that in your life and to adorn you with that. He has the power to make it happen.

Verse(s)	What godliness looks like
v. 1	Respect and submit to authorities.
v. 1	Be obedient to God.
vv. 1, 8, 14	Be devoted to doing whatever is good.
v. 2	Be peaceable and considerate, treating others with gentleness.
v. 9	Avoid foolish controversies or arguments.
v. 14	Be productive in providing for the urgent needs of others

Respond to the Lord about what you learned today.

Day Four Study—Adorning Yourself with Godliness

At the beginning of this study, you were challenged with this:

> What could be a more beautiful, worthwhile goal than to aspire to adorn yourself with godliness…to put yourself in order with the very character of God…to arrange or live your life properly displaying the beliefs you claim to profess…to dress, act, and be like Him for Him!

That was our hope for you as you learned from God's Word through these two letters.

Remember our definition of godliness: ***devotion to God expressed in a life that is pleasing to Him.*** In that, we take on His likeness—Godlikeness, not becoming God but presenting Him.

We adorn ourselves with godliness for God the Father and Jesus Christ because of our love for them and gratitude for what they have done for our salvation (1 Timothy 4:10). We adorn ourselves with godliness for ourselves and our fellow Christians because godly behavior is good for us in every way (1 Timothy 6:6, 19; Titus 2:11-13). And, as Titus 2:10 says, our adorning ourselves with godliness makes the teaching about Christ attractive and draws unbelievers to the God we know and serve.

We hoped that you would see who you really are and then "dress" in such a way to let others see your devotion to God expressed in a life that is pleasing to Him.

In what ways have you chosen to adorn yourself with godliness through this study?

> **Recommended**: Listen to the podcast "The Gospel: God's Cure for Our Fatal Sin Disease" after doing this lesson to reinforce what you have learned. Use the following listener guide.

The Gospel: God's Cure for Our Fatal Sin Disease

CHRIST'S FINISHED WORK ON THE CROSS

As a direct result of Christ's finished work on the cross, our relationship with God is changed because of our faith in Jesus Christ. What Jesus's death on the cross accomplished for us are described by six truths we can know and claim for ourselves. They are gifts of the cross for us.

Word of the Cross #1 is Propitiation.

- God's holy wrath against all sin is fully satisfied by Jesus's sacrifice on the cross. Because of that, God is able to extend mercy to every believer in Christ. There is no longer any sacrifice that anyone can ever do to satisfy God's wrath against sin apart from what Christ has already done. It's done, finished! *Romans 5:9*

- Because you've trusted Christ and are now found in Christ, you can know and live with confidence that God is satisfied and no longer angry at your sin—ever!

Word of the Cross #2 is Reconciliation.

- God restored our broken relationship with Him by reconciling us to Himself through Jesus's death on the cross. God chose to do that out of His love for us. *Romans 5:10*

- Because you've trusted Christ and are now found in Christ, you can know and live with confidence that your relationship with God is restored and no longer broken.

Word of the Cross #3 is Redemption.

- Every human born on this planet is born into bondage to "the kingdom of darkness" and a "slave to sin." Jesus paid the ransom price for you to be released from that bondage. When you trust in Jesus, you become the possession of a loving, merciful God and are able to live a life that pleases God. *Colossians 1:13; Romans 6*

- Because you've trusted Christ and are now found in Christ, you can know and live with confidence that you've been released and are no longer in bondage to sin and guilt.

Word of the Cross #4 is Forgiveness.

- God stepped in and did for us what we couldn't do for ourselves. He transferred our sin to a substitute, Jesus, and it was taken away—all of it from the time you were born through the time of your death has been canceled. As an already forgiven Christian, you can go through the biblical process for dealing with recognized sin. (See the podcast for Lesson 9). *Colossians 2:14*

- Because you've trusted Christ and are now found in Christ, you can know and live with confidence that you've been forgiven and are no longer burdened by your sin and guilt.

Word of the Cross #5 is Justification.

- Because of Christ's finished work on the cross, God chooses to give a "not guilty" status to anyone who places their faith in Jesus Christ. Then, you get His righteousness. When God looks on you, He sees His Son's righteousness taking the place of your sin—even your sin after you've been a believer for a long time. *Colossians 1:22*

- Because you've trusted Christ and are now found in Christ, you can know and live with confidence that you've been declared righteous and are no longer guilty of your sin.

Word of the Cross #6 is Sanctification.

- By faith in Jesus Christ, God declares us holy in His sight. Every believer has been set apart as God's special, beloved possession for His exclusive use. You are also "being made holy" in your thoughts, words, and actions by the Holy Spirit so that we become in thought and behavior what we are in status—holy as God is holy. Colossians 3

- Because you've trusted in Christ and are now found in Him, you can know and live with confidence that you are set apart by God, for God. In His eyes, you are perfected and no longer flawed.

CHRIST'S RESURRECTION—OUR REGENERATION

- Christ's resurrection opened the way for you to get new life that would never be taken away again because of your sin. That's "regeneration" and refers to the "restoration of spiritual life to one who is spiritually dead." *Ephesians 2:5; 2 Corinthians 5:17*

- We get this new life at the moment of salvation the Holy Spirit indwells us. We, who were once dead, are made alive by the indwelling Holy Spirit who unites you to Christ so that "Christ in you" is a fact of your new existence. *Colossians 1:27*

- Because you've trusted in Christ and are now found in Him, you can know and live with confidence that God's life is now indwelling you forever. You are made alive and no longer dead.

- This begins a new adventure of learning how to live with Christ in you and depending upon Him to do anything of value in your life. We can adorn ourselves with godliness because we have the life of Christ in us.

What could be a more beautiful, worthwhile goal than to adorn yourself with godliness ... to put yourself in order with the very character of God ... to arrange to live your life properly displaying the beliefs you claim to profess ... to dress, act, and be like Him for Him!

Let Jesus satisfy your heart with such love for God that you will want to live a life that pleases Him.

Small Group Discussion Guide

The following guide is designed for groups that meet for less than 1½ hours. You will notice that some questions are skipped for the sake of time.

Tell them how to find the podcasts (melanienewton.com/podcasts or any podcast platform—search "Satisfied" by Melanie Newton, Season 14: 1 Timothy / Titus. Or you can read the blogs associated with the podcasts at melanienewton.com/blog. Choose 1 Timothy / Titus category then scroll to find the title you want.

LESSON 1: INTRODUCTION TO 1 TIMOTHY AND TITUS

Choose ahead of time which verses from the questions the group will read aloud as you proceed through the discussion.

Start with prayer.

Icebreaker: Share your name, where you live, and one thing you would like the group to know about you.

Ask: Did anything grab your attention from the introductory podcast?

Day One

- Qs 1 & 2.
- Review the definition of godliness.

Day Two Study

- Qs 3 & 4.
- Qs 5 & 6.
- Read the "Scriptural Insight" together.

Day Three Study

- Qs 7 & 8.
- Q 10.

Day Four Study

- Have readers set to read selected verses.
- Qs 11- & 12.
- Q 13. Have one person read the 2 Peter verses and answer the questions. Same thing for the 1 Timothy verses. Do the rest separately.
- Read "Think About It."
- Qs 14 & 15.
- Discuss the podcast.
- Suggest they do Days 1, 3 and 4 before doing Day 2 to make sure they get to those last two sections about women.

> **Recommendation:** *Listen to a worship song such as "Speak, O Lord" by Keith and Kristen Getty, which fits very well with this study.*

LESSON 2: DRESSED IN TRUTH THAT STRENGTHENS DEVOTION TO GOD

Always read the main passage. Choose ahead of time which other verses from the questions the group will read aloud as you proceed through the discussion.

Start with prayer.

Icebreaker: What is your favorite piece of clothing and why is it your favorite?

Day One

- Q 1 & your choice of Qs 2-4.
- Ask which verse they chose for Q 5.

Day Two Study

- Read 1 Timothy 1:1-2 12-17.
- Discuss "Historical Insight."
- Q 6.
- Review the definition of godliness.
- Q 9—choose the ones you want to ask.
- Qs 11-13 and "Focus on the Meaning."
- Qs 15 & 16.
- Q 17 if you have time.

Day Three Study

- Read 1 Timothy 1:3-7 and 4:1-2.
- Q 18 and "Focus on the Meaning."
- Qs 20-22 and "Think About It" after Q 22.
- Read 1 Timothy 1:18-20.
- Qs 23 & 24 and "Historical Insight."
- Q 26.

Day Four Study

- Read 1 Timothy 1:7-11.
- Q 27 and "Scriptural Insight" after Q 28.
- Q 29.
- Qs 31-33.
- Q 34 if time.
- Discuss the podcast.

Recommendation: *Listen to a worship song such as "Speak, O Lord" by Keith and Kristen Getty, which fits very well with this study.*

LESSON 3: DRESSED FOR WORSHIPING GOD IN COMMUNITY

Always read the main passage. Choose ahead of time which other verses from the questions the group will read aloud as you proceed through the discussion.

Start with prayer.

Icebreaker: How long does it take for you to adorn yourself in the morning?

Day One

- Q 1 & your choice of Qs 2-5.
- Ask which verse they chose for Q 6.

Day Two Study

- Read 1 Timothy 2:1-10.
- Qs 7 & 8 plus the "Historical Insight" and "From the Greek."
- Do Qs 9-12 if you have lots of time.

Day Three Study

- Read 1 Timothy 2:8-10.
- Read the setting paragraph.
- Qs 13 & 14. Don't spend much time on these.
- Read the paragraphs before Q 16.
- Qs 16-18 and "Focus on the Meaning" after Q 18.
- Q 19.
- Q 21.

Day Four Study

- Read 1 Timothy 2:11-15 and "From the Greek."
- Qs 23 & 24 and "Scriptural Insight."
- Qs 25 & 26 and "Scriptural Insight."
- Q 27 and "Think About It."
- Q 29 and "Scriptural Insight."
- Discuss possible interpretations of verse 15 (first part), especially what it cannot mean.
- Qs 30 & 31 (if time).
- Discuss the podcast.

Recommendation: *Listen to a worship song such as "Speak, O Lord" by Keith and Kristen Getty, which fits very well with this study.*

LESSON 4: THE FABRIC FOR SERVANT-LEADERSHIP

Always read the main passage. Choose ahead of time which other verses from the questions the group will read aloud as you proceed through the discussion.

Start with prayer.

Icebreaker: Would you rather be a follower or a leader?

Day One

- Q 1 & your choice of Qs 2-5.
- Ask which verse they chose for Q 6.

Day Two Study

- Read 1 Timothy 3:1-7.
- Q 7 and read Mark 10:42-45.
- Skip Q 8.
- Read "Scriptura Insight" after Q 8.
- Qs 9 & 10.
- Qs 11 & 12.
- Q 14 if time.

Day Three Study

- Read 1 Timothy 3:8-13.
- Skip Q 15.
- Read paragraph after Q 15 and "Scriptural Insight."
- Qs 16 & 17 and "Focus on the Meaning."
- Q 20.
- Q 21.

Day Four Study

- Read 1 Timothy 3:14-16.
- Q 23 and "Think About It."
- Qs 26 & 27.
- Discuss the podcast.

Recommendation: *Listen to a worship song such as "Speak, O Lord" by Keith and Kristen Getty, which fits very well with this study.*

LESSON 5: DESIRING TO LOOK YOUR BEST

Always read the main passage. Choose ahead of time which other verses from the questions the group will read aloud as you proceed through the discussion.

Start with prayer.

Icebreaker: When have you heard that would be considered an "old wives' tale" today?

Day One

- Q 1 & your choice of Qs 2-5.
- Ask which verse they chose for Q 6.

Day Two Study

- Read 1 Timothy 4:1-6.
- Q 8. Read the paragraph about Q 9.
- Q 9. Read 2 Timothy 4:3-4. Read "Think About It."
- Q 10.
- Qs 11 & 12.

Day Three Study

- Read 1 Timothy 4:7-10.
- Q 13 and "Focus on the Meaning."
- Q 15. Read 2 Peter 1:3. Discuss "Think About It."
- Q 16.
- Q 17 third bullet point especially.

Day Four Study

- Read 1 Timothy 4:11-16.
- Qs 18-22.
- Q 23.
- Read "Think About It."
- Qs 25 & 26. Discuss the "Dependent Living" process.
- Q 27 if time.
- Discuss the podcast. Point out the destructive nature of legalism and how God's grace is what should motivate us to obedience because of our love and gratitude.

Recommendation: *Listen to a worship song such as "Speak, O Lord" by Keith and Kristen Getty, which fits very well with this study.*

LESSON 6: CLOTHING RELATIONSHIPS WITH RESPECT

Always read the main passage. Choose ahead of time which other verses from the questions the group will read aloud as you proceed through the discussion.

Start with prayer.

Icebreaker: What do you appreciate about being created by God as a woman?

Day One

- Q 1 & your choice of Qs 2-5.

Day Two Study

- Read 1 Timothy 5:1-8 and 16. Summarize the two paragraphs.
- Qs 7-9.
- Qs 11 & 12 and "Scriptural Insight."
- Q 13 first bullet.

Day Three Study

- Read 1 Timothy 5:9-10 and "Historical Insight."
- Q 14 and paragraph after Q 15.
- Qs 16-20.
- Q 21.

Day Four Study

- Read 1 Timothy 5:11-15. Summarize next paragraph.
- Q 22 and "Focus on the Meaning."
- Q 23 and "Focus on the Meaning."
- Qs 24-26 "Think About It."
- Qs 29-30.
- Discuss the podcast. Point out why women in the same family might have difficulty caring for one another. Also, point out how God has given us social skills to benefit the body of Christ.

Recommendation: *Listen to a worship song such as "Speak, O Lord" by Keith and Kristen Getty, which fits very well with this study.*

LESSON 7: REPUTATION AND RESOURCES

Always read the main passage. Choose ahead of time which other verses from the questions the group will read aloud as you proceed through the discussion.

Start with prayer.

Icebreaker: When are you most likely to feel content?

Day One

- Q 1 & your choice of Qs 2-5.
- Ask which verse they chose for Q 6.

Day Two Study

- Read 1 Timothy 5:17-22.
- Q 8.
- Q 9-10.
- Q 11.
- Q 12 general discussion.

Day Three Study

- Read 1 Timothy 5:23-6:2.
- Q 13.
- Comments about information before Q 14.
- Q 14. Summarize what they learned.
- Read "Dependent Living."
- Q 15.
- Qs 17-18. Read either "Think About It' if appropriate for your group.
- Q 19. General discussion.

Day Four Study

- Read 1 Timothy 6:3-10.
- Qs 20-21.
- Q 22. State answer to 1st bullet and ask 2nd bullet.
- Qs 23 and 25.
- Qs 26-27.
- Qs 29-30.
- Discuss the podcast.

Recommendation: *Listen to a worship song such as "Speak, O Lord" by Keith and Kristen Getty, which fits very well with this study.*

LESSON 8: PURSUE GODLINESS

Always read the main passage. Choose ahead of time which other verses from the questions the group will read aloud as you proceed through the discussion.

Start with prayer.

Icebreaker: Today's passage is full of action words. What 3 actions did you take yesterday that moved you forward in some area?

Day One

- Qs 1 & 5.
- Ask which verse they chose for Q 6.

Day Two Study

- Read 1 Timothy 6:11-16.
- Qs 7-8 and "Focus on the Meaning."
- Q 9 and "Focus on the Meaning."
- Q 10. Summarize 1st and 2nd bullets. Ask 3rd bullet question.
- Q 11.
- Q 13. Consider doing the "Think About It." That is one way to fight the good fight of faith.
- Q 14 for those who have something to share. Read "Think About It."

Day Three Study

- Read 1 Timothy 6:17-21.
- Qs 15-18. Read "Think About It" after Q 15 and Q 18.
- Q 19 and "Dependent Living" that follows.
- Q 20.

Day Four Study

- Qs 22-23. Read "From the Greek."
- Q 25.
- Q 26.
- Discuss the podcast.

Recommendation: *Listen to a worship song such as "Speak, O Lord" by Keith and Kristen Getty, which fits very well with this study.*

LESSON 9: BEING KNOWN BY YOUR ACTIONS

Always read the main passage. Choose ahead of time which other verses from the questions the group will read aloud as you proceed through the discussion.

Start with prayer.

Icebreaker: What is one thing for which you are known by others?

Day One

- Q 1 & Q 2.

Day Two Study

- Q 3 and your choice of Qs 2-5.
- Ask which verse they chose for Q 8.

Day Three Study

- Read Titus 1:1-5.
- Q 9 and "Focus on the Meaning"
- Qs 10 & 11
- Q 12: ask if anyone did this. Notice how consistent Paul was with this.
- Qs 13 & 14
- Q 16, especially second bullet so you can pray for each other.

Day Four Study

- Read Titus 1:6-16.
- Summarize information after "What does it mean?"
- Q 17 (all)
- Q 18
- Qs 20 & 21
- Qs 22 & 23 if that applies to your group
- Discuss the podcast.

Recommendation: *Listen to a worship song such as "Speak, O Lord" by Keith and Kristen Getty, which fits very well with this study.*

LESSON 10: ADORN YOURSELF WITH GODLINESS IN RELATIONSHIPS

Always read the main passage. Choose ahead of time which other verses from the questions the group will read aloud as you proceed through the discussion.

Start with prayer.

Icebreaker: What one thing have you learned from an older woman that has benefited you?

Day One

- Q 1 & your choice of Qs 2-6.

Day Two Study

- Read Titus 2:1-6.

- Read the paragraphs before Q7 and discuss Q 7.

- Qs 8-10, including "From the Greek" and "Focus on the Meaning."

- Qs 11-14.

Day Three Study

- Read Titus 2:7-10.

- Q 15.

- Qs 17 & 18 and "Think About It."

- Qs 19 & 20.

Day Four Study

- Read Titus 2:11-15.

- Skip Q21. Read the information below "What does it mean?"

- Qs 22-25 and "Think About It" after Q 25.

- Qs 27-28 if time.

- Discuss the podcast.

Recommendation: *Listen to a worship song such as "Speak, O Lord" by Keith and Kristen Getty, which fits very well with this study.*

LESSON 11: LIVING IN RESPONSE TO GOD'S GRACE

Always read the main passage. Choose ahead of time which other verses from the questions the group will read aloud as you proceed through the discussion.

Start with prayer.

Icebreaker: How old were you when you understood the gospel and knew you were saved?

Day One

- Q 1 & your choice of Qs 2-6.

Day Two Study

- Read Titus 3:1-7.
- Qs 7-11.
- Q 13.

Day Three Study

- Read Titus 3:8-15.
- Qs 14-16 and "Historical Insight."
- Qs 18 & 19.
- Q 20, if desired.

Day Four Study

- Read and share.
- Discuss the podcast.

Recommendation: *Listen to a worship song such as "Speak, O Lord" by Keith and Kristen Getty, which fits very well with this study.*

Sources

1. *Crown Ministries Small Group Financial Study*
2. *Dr. Constable's Notes on 1 Timothy 2020 Edition*
3. *Dr. Constable's Notes on Titus 2020 Edition*
4. Irving L. Jensen, *1 & 2 Timothy and Titus, A Self-Study Guide*
5. J. Vernon McGee, *Thru-the-Bible Commentary Series*
6. Jerry Bridges, *The Practice of Godliness*
7. John Foxe, *Foxe's Book of Martyrs*
8. John Stott, *Fighting the Good Fight*
9. *Life Application Bible Study Guide, 1 & 2 Timothy & Titus*
10. Quotes from Chuck Swindoll and C. S. Lewis
11. *Titus Lifechange Series Bible Study*
12. *Vines Complete Expository Dictionary of Old and New Testament Words*
13. Walvoord and Zuck, *The Bible Knowledge Commentary (New Testament)*